The State

Concepts in Social Thought

Series Editor: Frank Parkin

Concepts in Social Thought

The State

*John A. Hall and
G. John Ikenberry*

University of Minnesota Press

Minneapolis

Published by the University of Minnesota Press
2037 University Avenue Southeast, Minneapolis MN 55414
Published simultaneously in Canada
by Fitzhenry & Whiteside Limited, Markham.

Printed in Great Britain

JC
325
. H26
1989

Library of Congress Cataloging-in-Publication Data
Hall, John A., 1949–
  The state/John A. Hall and G. John Ikenberry.
      p.   cm. – (Concepts in social thought)
  Bibliography: p.
  Includes index.
  ISBN 0–8166–1795–3   ISBN 0–8166–1796–1 (pbk.)
  1. State, The.   I. Ikenberry, G. John.   II. Title.   III. Series.
JC325.H26   1989   89–30846
320.1 – dc19   CIP

R00701 32762

The University of Minnesota
is an equal-opportunity
educator and employer.

Contents

Acknowledgements

Most of our principal intellectual debts are obvious from the text. In addition, however, we want to thank the following friends and colleagues, all of whom helped significantly in the preparation of this book: Michael Doyle, Jeff Goodwin, David Spiro, Stephan Haggard, Valerie Kanka, Mary Waters, David Lake, Michael Mann, Theda Skocpol, and Caroline Thomas.

Introduction: The State and Social Theory

The period in which social science 'lost interest' in the state – broadly speaking, those years in which the liberal *Pax Americana* dominated minds as much as institutions – is now over. The return of scholarly concern with the state led initially to several rather programmatic statements, many of which were formidably obscure.[1] Happily we are now better placed. It is easy, with the advantage of a decade of state-centred social science explanations behind us, to demonstrate the impact of the state. What is harder but now possible is the creation of a more systematic view of the state in history. Our general aim is to specify the ways in which states interact with other sources of power; the fact that the character of those power sources has varied in history requires a proper treatment of the state to have an historical dimension. We are particularly concerned with the relationship between states and capitalism, and in the ways in which this affects political regimes and the stability of the international system. But before beginning to trace the state's relationship with other power sources, we need to devote considerable space to views of the state in classical and contemporary social theory. This will give our account greater richness. More importantly, our historically-grounded analysis will enable us to look back at these theoretical traditions and to adjudicate their claims.

The state defined

There is a great deal of agreement amongst social scientists as to how the state should be defined.[2] A composite definition would include three elements. First, the state is a set of institutions; these are manned by the state's own personnel. The state's most important institution is that of the means of violence and coercion. Second, these institutions are at the centre of a geographically-bounded territory, usually referred to as a society. Crucially, the state looks inwards to its national society and outwards to larger societies in which it must make its way; its behaviour in one area can often only be explained by its activities in the other. Third, the state monopolises rule making within its territory. This tends towards the creation of a common political culture shared by all citizens.

No definition is perfect; some comments on the limitations of this one are in order. Note immediately that the definition is at once institutional and functional. History sometimes makes it necessary to decouple this linkage. Thus in Latin Christendom in the early European Middle Ages, many governmental functions – the provision of order, rules of war and justice – were provided by the Church rather than by the puny and transient states which existed within its boundaries.[3] To make this point implicitly reveals a very great deal about the nature of our definition. Not all societies in history have been controlled by a state. Chinese civilization was *usually* controlled by a single state, but Latin Christendom was *never* so controlled; modern capitalist society, within whose boundaries most states now live, clearly has laws of development all its own. Furthermore, states do not always possess complete control over the means of violence, as feudal rulers knew all too well. Equally obviously, it is not the case that those over whom states rule always share a single culture. The conclusion to be drawn from this is simple: fully-fledged 'stateness' has been an aspiration for *every* state in history.[4] In consequence, the word 'tends' which is now in the third proposition of the composite definition above could be appended to virtually every statement in the definition. Some states have moved a considerable way from aspiration towards achieve-ment; this was especially true of European states at the turn of the century, as is evidenced by the fact that this composite definition is based upon statements of their social scientists.[5] Most states of the contemporary Third World, in contrast, comprise hope more than reality: their citizens often do not belong to a single culture, that is, they are not yet nation states, and they are only in the earliest stages of creating an apparatus of state machinery.

It is important to highlight how complex is the notion of society used so far. Social organizations and social identities may be larger than the boundaries of states and may have some power over them; equally the state may not be able to control all social groups which exist inside its own territory. In general, state power has gained as other sources of power, notably ideological and military power, have been territorialized. We pay great attention in this book to the relations of states to capitalism because it has proved far harder for states to territorialize economic power. This statement should not be read naively: if the extensiveness of capitalism means that the state's search for security is not total and complete, states do have the possibility, if they can organize their citizenries, of enhancing their position *through* acquiring the wealth that participation in the global economy can bring.

Classical approaches to the state

Three classical theories, liberalism, Marxism and realism, have made the most important contributions to understanding the state. We examine them in turn, paying particular attention to their views of the state as a force within society and as a social actor in external interactions with a larger world.

Liberalism

Liberalism is a protean doctrine, but its core idea is extremely simple: the individual is held to be the seat of moral worth.[6] State activities *inside* a society were seen by liberals in more or less sophisticated ways. A notably sophisticated view was that of Adam Smith. In the third book of the *Wealth of Nations* he described the manner in which the spread of commerce, by allowing the feudal aristocracy to spend its money on commodities rather than on retainers, allowed for the emergence of the rule of law. The causal chain of Smith's argument was complex and subtle: it was the parcellization of sovereignty that took place upon the fall of Rome, that is to say, a political factor, which gave birth to the autonomous and productive city whose economic impact in undermining feudal power was so great. This undermining was clearly welcomed by Smith in and of itself.[7] This theory of liberalism realized fully that power has its own attractions, is capable of being abused and stands in permanent need of being controlled. In other words, commercial society was praised on the instrumental ground that it allowed for a decent political system by replacing naked power with *le doux commerce*.[8]

Adam Smith is best known, however, for his insistence – made as the last proposition of the causal chain of social development he had discovered – that a certain type of state, a minimalist 'night-watchman', provided the best shell for economic growth. 'Little else is requisite,' he apparently believed, 'to carry a state to the highest degree of opulence from the lowest barbarism, but peace, easy taxes, and a tolerable administration of justice; all the rest being brought about by the natural course of things.'[9] It was this injunction, divorced from the full context of Smith's argument, that became reified in the nineteenth century, particularly by Herbert Spencer. This view was less sophisticated than its predecessor because it simply equated capitalism with liberalism, rather than seeing the former as a means to the latter. Spencer's greatest hope was that the state would cease to exist: fully developed individuals would consort together without benefit of any constraint whatever, this being beneficial to their moral fibre as well as helpful for the market principle. Smith was some way removed from this anti-political view. As noted, he had a more realistic appreciation of the need to control power. Importantly, this did not lead him to seek to abolish the state; for 'peace' and the 'administration of justice' allow for a more substantial state presence than is often realized. Furthermore, a wise political elite was necessary in order that the selfish demands of leading capitalists, keen to feather their own nests by monopolies even at the cost of destroying the beneficial and dynamic workings of the market, were to be resisted.[10] Scarcely known at all is the fact that Smith was well aware that the market principle in European history could be unleashed, once the blocking powers of state interference had been removed, only because the human *matériel* was of the right type:

> . . . it was the general diffusion of wealth among the lower orders of men, which first gave birth to the spirit of independence in modern Europe, and which has produced under some of its governments, and especially under our own, a more equal diffusion of freedom and of happiness than took place under the most celebrated constitutions of antiquity.[11]

Liberal thinkers were well aware that states had gained much of their salience from their *external* activities. The most sophisticated thinker of the liberal tradition in this respect, then and since, is Immanuel Kant. His 'Perpetual Peace' is characterized by a remarkable realism, that is, he accepted that the state, given the 'asocial society' of European international relations, was a necessary instrument of security, but he nevertheless produced a plan to encourage peace. If states had liberal governments, opened themselves to outsiders and encouraged trade with other similar states in a liberal league, then peace would follow; those who might be killed in war would restrain governments, while a general awareness that the mutual advantages of interlinked trade would be destroyed by war would prove as important. One difficulty with Kant's argument is that it is hard to specify precisely which factor is preventing war; another is the suspicion that a liberal state might see a non-liberal rival as a total affront to its way of life – something which could actually intensify geopolitical conflict.[12]

It was the last of Kant's conditions – that concerning the pacific tendencies of international trade – that came to dominate liberalism in the nineteenth century. Capitalist theory in general maintained that even rich states would benefit from the development, by means of comparative advantage, of poorer ones: provided rich states were flexible enough to move to production based on capital and skill, there was no reason why the market should not expand in such a manner as to allow all states to prosper at the same time. Thinkers such as Richard Cobden and John Bright insisted in consequence that an interdependent world could be created in which prosperity would be attainable for all. Wars were no longer rational: the age of scarcity had ended, and it was at last possible for peace and prosperity to reign. This noble vision was, of course, profoundly anti-political. Cobden's favourite toast was 'No foreign politics'; his views were neatly captured in a parliamentary speech:

> The progress of freedom depends more upon the maintenance of peace, the spread of commerce, and the diffusion of education, than upon the labours of cabinets and foreign offices . . . [There should be] as little intercourse as possible between Governments; as much connexion as possible between the nations of the world.[13]

This led Cobden and Bright to oppose all interventions, even to the extent of being resistant both to balance of power considerations and to nationalist calls for help in the struggle of peoples to be free. Not all liberals were as consistent; the foreign policy of the Liberal Party under Gladstone, for example, operated according to rather traditional principles – with the exception that occupations, no-tably that of Egypt, were justified on the 'moral' ground that they would help raise up barbarians who could then take their place amongst the nations of the world. None the less, the desire to abolish war, largely by curtailing the independence of individual states, has remained a strong one; it was seen at its most powerful in the aftermath of the First World War in the creation of the League of Nations.

There will be occasion later to analyse the extent to which liberalism has been able, within the terms of its general ethic, to explain the incidence of two world wars. However, the very nub of liberalism's explanation for a revival of geopolitical struggle deserves to be noted here. It is classically expressed in John Hobson's famous *Imperialism*. Hobson was writing as a liberal who disliked the move from the informal imperialism of free trade to the formal acquisition of territory demanded by the 'new imperialism' of the end of the nineteenth century. He was sufficiently aware of the realities of international economics to realize that imperial possessions were usually expensive, and a dreadful drain on resources – an argument amply supported by modern scholarship. The trouble with this rationalist argument against imperialism is that it failed to explain the South African war against the Boers. If imperialism was economically irrational, did this not mean that social actors were being utterly irrational, incapable of calculating their own interests? If that were true, did it not signal the end of all liberal hopes? Hobson rejected this pessimism on the grounds that the war could be explained in rational terms. What was not rational for the nation and the business community as a whole *was* in the interests of a particular section of the business community.[14] The interests in question were those of international, and Jewish, finance. These interests depended upon the excessive profits that resulted from an underconsumptionist economy – an economy in which there was an unjust and unwise distribution of income. All this was comforting to Hobson: war was still explicable in social terms, and it was still unnecessary in the modern world – provided that the capitalist economy were slightly modified.

Marxism

To fight an enemy influences one's own mind. To no thinker does this maxim apply with more force than to Karl Marx. *Capital* was a critique of political economy, and this led to Marx's thought sharing key presuppositions with liberalism, the most important of which will be noted in a moment. But Marxism is larger than Marx himself, and crucial differences between it and liberalism will be noted. In general, Marx's thought is more attractive, even nobler, than that of his descendants; it is also sociologically naive.

The fundamental difference between the thought of Marx and that of classical liberalism concerns class. Marx insisted that those political citizenship rights given prominence by the revolutionaries in France were not in themselves sufficient to guarantee generalised human freedom. What mattered more than the universal right to vote was the inequality established between those who owned the means of production and those who, without such means, were forced to labour for them. The fundamental notion of the state, a notion concerned with its *internal* workings, in Marx's work follows from this. The state is not at any time a neutral force, representing the general interest. On the contrary, the state embodies the interests of the dominant class; the rules that it produces correspondingly serve the interests of some rather than all of the people.[15]

As is well known, Marx had occasion to go beyond this form of extreme societal reductionism, itself so similar to the naiver form of liberalism. In *The Eighteenth Brumaire of Louis Bonaparte*, he suggested that the state might gain 'relative autonomy' by being able to balance between competing fragments of the ruling class.[16] This analysis has taken on canonical status for many contemporary Western Marxists, especially when they seek to explain the modern welfare state – the mere existence of which seemingly contradicts Marxism. Such theorists argue that the relative autonomy of the state allows it to force through welfare measures which are in the long-term interest of capital, both so as to ensure stability and so as to create a skilled and productive work-force. None the less, Marxists continue to stress that class conflict will eventually allow for the 'withering away of the state' – an all too faithful wording of Spencer's liberal dream. Marx entertained the notion that a dictatorship of the proletariat might be necessary during the final stages of class struggle, and Stalin added to this the belief that the class struggle intensifies towards its end; but the recognition that a revolutionary state might fully centralize power did not stand in the way of the fantastic notion that such states would then seek to abolish themselves. According to this view, the state has no fundamental reality in itself, and it is therefore not necessary to think about ways in which political power can be controlled.

Marx expected that capitalism would be destroyed within the

foreseeable future as the result of the activities of the working class itself. It is puzzling that Marx did not follow Hegel in stressing that the *external* activities of the advanced states, and in particular their drive for empire, might stave off revolutionary change.[17] As it was, Marx's conceptual apparatus really has no place at all for the external activities of states. Classes were considered to be transnational within his system of thought, and it was this legacy that made members of the Second International arrive at their famous meeting in 1914 presuming that the working class as a whole would not fight in what was held to be a capitalist war.

Friedrich Engels had some premonition of the great destruction that industrial war would bring.[18] None the less, it was Lenin who provided a fully developed alternative within Marxism to Marx's own thought on these matters.[19] Lenin's fundamental achievement was to recognize that states lived within capitalist society. What concerned him most about this was the way in which, in his view, the needs of different national capitalisms led naturally to geopolitical conflict. His argument sought to explain the origins of the First World War in terms of displaced colonial rivalries. Lenin differed from Hobson in having no belief that the capitalist home market might be expanded sufficiently to absorb excess production; he regarded the search for markets as absolutely inherent to the nature of capitalism.

In one sense, Lenin's argument is scarcely Marxist at all: it admits the prior importance of states. However, a fundamental Marxist orientation can be maintained by insisting that each European state was driven into particular actions because it was controlled or influenced by its national capitalists. It is worth highlighting that what lies at the back of this line of Marxist argumentation is a simple, unsettling and profound observation. Capitalism develops unevenly throughout the globe. The desire to break into established markets on the part of a particular set of national capitalists leads, according to this scenario, to the outbreak of war. And this Lenin welcomed. For by 1917 he had come to believe that socialism was most likely to be established in that situation of fluidity, marked, above all, by a collapse of state coercive forces, that followed defeat in war.[20]

It is necessary to make a slight digression at this point. Lenin's theory was dynamic, just as Marx's theory of the class relations internal to a capitalist society had been. But there are Marxist writers who have produced static, functionalist theories. Many such theories seek to account for the failure of workers to behave in the requisite revolutionary manner. In recent years, one striking theory of this sort focusing on external relations has received much attention. Theorists of capitalism as a world system have suggested that the 'core' of the capitalist economy systematically exploits the 'peripheral' regions of the world.[21] Lenin's point had effectively been that the core of capitalism does not stay in the same place, and that rising states, representing their capitalists, can mount a challenge to any particular ordering of the world political economy. While there is nothing in world systems theory to rule out recognition of such processes, the main drive of its theorists, and particularly those seeking to explain the 'dependency' of the contemporary Third World, has been to suggest that the exploitative relations between core and periphery will be fixed and stable. Such theorists follow the lead of Karl Kautsky, who argued against Lenin on the grounds that capitalists would be intelligent enough to patch up the differences that stood between them.

Realism

There is a fundamental similarity between the way in which liberalism and Marxism view the state: both see it as a secondary phenomenon, and deem its character and drive to result from the impact of societal forces upon it. In contrast, those thinkers we pull together here, perhaps arbitrarily, as realists do not share this view at all. These are statist thinkers in a pure sense.

In regard to the *internal* workings of the state, realists insist that the provision of order, that is, the prevention of predation and terror, is a good in every sense. While it is true that a state can become a monster in its own right, as both the Assyrians and Pol Pot proved, it is worth remembering that Hobbes's most basic point was that peace was necessary in order that production, exchange and prosperity could then follow.[22] More generally, realists point out that notions of abolishing the state, on the part of extreme liberals, past or present, and Marxists, only really make sense in nation states which have high standards of public order. Liberal thinkers thus fail to see that the abolition of the state can lead to a reversion to the jungle, as in Beirut and Belfast. It is perhaps not surprising that the sense of loyalty shown to a state, and more particularly a nation state, tends to be much more powerful than that shown towards more obscure transnational ideologies such as Marxism and liberalism. The presence of a state allows for peace in social relations within societies.

The importance of the state's provision of order can be seen most clearly in the developing world. The task which Third World countries face is one of national state-building; a stronger state presence is required for security reasons, to establish order and to create the proper human *matériel* without which modernization is impossible.[23] Others have noted the centrality of the state in industrialization itself. The continental European countries that followed England in the path of economic development found it necessary to forge elaborate institutional links between industry, banks, and the state bureaucracy. The 'late industrializers', as Alexander Gerschenkron describes Germany and Russia, were ill-equipped to confront already established foreign competitors; capital was scarce but the international pace of the industrialization movement put pressure on such late industrializing countries to develop large and productive enterprises.[24] Confronted with such circumstances, it was only natural that the state came to play a more direct role in industrial development.

It is, however, in the *external* realm that realism has made its greatest contribution to state theory, and indeed to social theory as a whole. The fundamental insight of the whole school is neatly captured in this passage from Hobbes:

> [Y]et in all times Kings, and Persons of Soveraign authority, because of their independency, are in continuable jealousies, and are in the state and posture of Gladiators; having their weapons pointing, and their eyes fixed on one another; that is, their Forts, Garrisons, and Guns, upon the Frontiers of their Kingdoms; and continuable spyes upon their neighbours; which is a posture of war.[25]

In its modern guise, realist scholars of international relations can agree on at least three arguments. First, political life is dominated by sovereign nation states, each beholden to no higher authority than itself. The international system, in a word, is anarchic. Second, the relations among states are fundamentally competitive, although this need not preclude the possibilities for co-operation when it suits the interests of particular states. Finally, with a system so constituted, nation states behave with purpose and direction, making choices that enhance the power and material well-being of their inhabitants.[26]

From these propositions a myriad of consequences follow. Most important of all, a state must try and calculate the intentions of other states. The search for security by a state means that, in a system of states, it will seek to play balance of power politics. It was in this spirit that Francis I allied himself with the Turks in order to control the imperial pretensions of Spain. It is possible, moreover, to produce geopolitical laws or propositions on the basis of the simple fact that the world polity, unlike a national society, has no single source of authority. It is normal, for example, to befriend the enemy of one's own enemy. But for appreciation of this maxim, it seems likely that Japan might have swallowed China, which the United States sought to protect, during the course of the 1930s. More generally, however, we can say that it is natural to expect, for example, an area of weak states to stand between those which are more powerful: such zones help warn of military attack. It is thus historically normal that Israel and Syria should find the condition of contemporary Lebanon to their advantage. None the less, such laws vary historically. Admiral Mahan's powerful insights into the role that sea power had played in European history, for example, became outdated just at the moment they were expressed, in large part due to the fact that the railway then became capable of mobilizing resources within large landmasses – a situation best theorized by Sir Halford Mackinder.[27]

The power of a state is very closely related to its wealth, and state strategies often seek to maximize the latter to gain the former. The classic doctrine expressing this position was mercantilism, and this enjoyed huge success in the late seventeenth and eighteenth centuries.[28] More recent work in this area is known as 'international political economy'. Realists stress that the initial drive for industrialization was provided by the state, and that this was very largely for reasons of its own military security. This disrupted liberal hopes that the hidden hand of economic growth would bring political harmony; the fact that there were military origins to industrialization – that each state wished to have its own militarily important industries – led to the creation of surpluses, which in turn encouraged international trade rivalry.[29] Recognition of such forces led, at the end of the Second World War, to the creation of a subset of realist theory which has gained the name 'hegemonic stability theory'.[30] According to this theory, industrial capitalist society is likely to work smoothly only when a single liberal great power, historically either Great Britain or the United States, performs certain functions for the system as a whole – most notably, those of providing a currency, exporting capital for development and absorbing surplus production. Discord in world politics is held to result from the fact that such hegemony has tended to be self-liquidating as the leading power becomes exhausted by providing an excessive share of necessary public goods. This seems to condemn us to endless cycles of wars, reconstructions and renewed geopolitical challenges as the uneven development of capitalism leads a rising state to challenge a world order reflecting the dominance of a fading great power.

A recent theoretical development

These classical traditions differ in their views of the nature of the state. The key difference concerns the composition of the state: are institutions and individuals within the state in some significant sense separate from society and capable of acting on behalf of 'state goals'? Liberal and Marxist approaches understand the state to be penetrated by classes or groups and, therefore, fundamentally reducible to forces that emanate from society. Realists generally find the state capable of acting more or less purposively in pursuit of larger economic or geopolitical goals; and they clearly regret those occasions on which the state is not autonomous, believing in particular that this adversely affects the conduct of foreign policy.[31]

It would, of course, be an important and significant finding if the rest of this book were to report that states really did not matter much. There will be occasions when there *is* something to be said for the view that the state is not everything; but we will in fact be able to locate and explain key moments when state power has affected the course of history. As it has already been asserted that the state is but one source of power in society, this claim will entail describing those occasions in which state actors were able to push other actors down particular historical paths. It is hard to locate such occasions because history is continuous and multi-causal – a state which acts decisively has often itself been previously moulded by social forces, just as the new situation it creates will draw to it the renewed attention of those other forces. But the task is by no means impossible. Our model in this approach can be Adam Smith's description of the interaction of politics and economics in the rise of commerce in European history.

Recent theorists of the state have principally been interested in the exact nature of state 'autonomy' – or, to use different terminologies, in the usefulness of drawing distinctions between 'strong' and 'weak' states and between those with or without much state 'capacity'.[32] These distinctions are really but a rewriting of the key concerns of classical social theory. However, there has recently been one novel theoretical development, and we want to pay particular attention to it. Michael Mann has argued that there are two dimensions, despotic and infrastructural, to state power.[33] The despotic power of the state is great when the state can act arbitrarily, free from constitutional constraint. However, the sound and fury of command means little if orders do not translate into reality. The infrastructural dimension of state power – the ability to penetrate society and to organize social relations – is quite as important. The character of this distinction will become ever more apparent during the course of this book. None the less, the very fact of this distinction allows us immediately to problematize and to deepen our understanding of the notions of state strength and autonomy; although these terms are not dropped hereafter, analytic clarity is enhanced by concentrating the greater part of our attention on the more aseptic concept of state capacity.

The fact that there are two dimensions to state power necessitates scepticism about states traditionally held to have been strong. The French absolutist state in the eighteenth century was not, for example, anything like as powerful as its constitutional British rival. It had a lesser infrastructural capacity to penetrate its society than did its British counterpart, despite its formally greater despotic powers. This was particularly obvious in its inability to tax its aristocracy, a crucial matter which largely accounts for France's poor record in inter-state competition with its main geopolitical rival. The conclusion to be emphasized is that the strength of a state depends greatly upon its ability to penetrate and organise society; the pretensions of despotism must not be taken at face value. A similar point can be made about the state in contemporary capitalist society. State intervention in society, initially indicative of capacity to shape internal political and economic practices, may eventually lead to commitments and obligations, especially with the creation of new and entrenched pressure groups, that bind the state in subsequent periods of decision. Ironically, the 'strong' state over time may become enfeebled by its own action and thereby begin to look quite 'weak'.[34] The best state industrial policy for advanced and liberal national capitalist societies is, as we shall see, to create a massive social infrastructure, of skill, knowledge, loans and communicative competence that allows citizens to adapt to market change rather than to manage industry directly.

We need to be equally wary of naive usage of the notion of state autonomy. We can best stress the general point by remembering that there are *two* classical definitions of power. If one is the zero-sum ability to force someone to do something, another equally valid tradition stresses the *powering* that can result when autonomous bodies co-operate, when different sources of energy contribute to a common goal. If freedom *from* societal pressure increases state autonomy in one sense, it is important to insist that working through the independent groups of civil society can increase state autonomy in the sense of its being *free* (or able) actually *to* generate the largest possible sum of social energy. Power can be increased when it is shared. Mann is mistaken in this context principally to consider infrastructural power as being held *over* society; on the contrary, such power can result more – as we will see when analysing early modern England and contemporary Japan – from the provision by the state of co-ordinating infrastructural services *for* society. An implication of all this is that totalitarian states which seek to control rather than to co-operate, preferring to rule over a socially atomized populace rather than to work with plural groups of an autonomous civil society, are not likely, in the final analysis, to be highly efficient generators of social energy.[35] One obvious consequence is to be drawn from the discovery that the state can be too distant from society as well as too constrained by it: gaining, exercising and maintaining state capacity is an extremely complicated matter, in which there will be a perpetual dialectic between the state seizing and being granted authority.[36] Historical and comparative studies have made us aware that state capacity is often the consequence of the state's position, at the head of a society faced with other societies. Clearly, extreme geopolitical pressure increases state capacity.[37] Equally, small countries in modern capitalist society have no choice but to develop state capacity in order to respond flexibly to the market by internal change; they do not have the option of larger states, better insulated from international economic shocks, and thereby tempted instead to seek to change the rules of international economic life.[38] However, there remains an ineluctable human element that goes beyond these structural considerations. State power depends, at least in part, upon the intelligence, nimbleness and skill of political actors: if social actors are given particular cards much depends upon the way they play them.

Conclusion

We have discussed the interrelations between states, political regimes, and capitalism; in this book empirical light will be cast on these issues. In a book of this length, it is simply not possible to spell out and consider every single question that results from the interweaving of these forces. But crucial issues can be addressed by focusing attention on historical episodes which have relevance for these theoretical debates. The first two episodes concern recognized historical breakthroughs. Chapter 2 offers an account of the origins of the state. Chapter 3 explains, in comparative perspective, what it was about the European state which allowed for the emergence of capitalism, itself the progenitor of that vast increase in human collective power we term 'industrialism'. Chapter 4 suggests that the institutional package which allowed that early dynamism contained within itself, at least in the industrial era it created, the seeds of its own destruction in world war. Chapter 5 asks simply if the nature of states and their interactions since 1945 has changed in any way that will allow us to escape a repetition of disaster. The final chapter returns to the theoretical issues outlined here.

The Origins of the State

Most of human history has not been graced by the presence of states. The fossil record shows traces of *Homo sapiens* 40,000 years ago, but the first really recognizable state only appears in Mesopotamia around 3000 BC. Such a dramatic change drew the attention of classical social theories. Both liberalism and Marxism have essentially evolutionary views of the origins of the state. They assert that a hunter-gatherer way of life became outmoded and was then replaced by that 'invention' of agriculture subsequently termed the 'neolithic revolution'; the greater social complexity that resulted, sometimes associated with a progression in terms of political organization from band to tribe, is held to have led to the creation of the state. Liberalism sees the emergence of the state in functional terms, as the creation of an organ to fulfil common purposes.[1] In contrast, Marxism – confronting the dreadful conceptual question as to what worm in the bud in egalitarian primitive society could have allowed for the birth of class in the first place – suggests that the state is made by, and for, the first recorded class of history. In contrast to these societal theories, German social theory, which stands much closer to realism, produced a simple and straightforward account of the emergence of the state. According to this view, best expressed by Ratzel, Oppenheimer, Gumplowicz and Thurnwald but present, too, in Max Weber and Eberhard, the state resulted from military conquest, often of a settled agricultural population by outlying nomads.[2]

None of these theories gains complete support from modern scholarship, although each possesses insights of occasional use. This scholarship has made a major advance in the manner of conceptualizing the origins of the state. None the less, it can be admitted that general agreement about the social processes involved in the

formation of the state is *never* likely to be forthcoming. The reason
for this is simple: there really are too few cases of the pristine, that
is, non-imitative, development of the state to allow firm generaliz-
ations. Certainly the state originated in this manner in Meso-
America and in Mesopotamia without any possibility of contact,
and the same is very probably true of the early states of the Indus
river valley, China and Peru; there may, however, have been some
sort of diffusion to Egypt. Diffusion marked most cases treated by
scholars discussing state origins; this means that those states are
secondary imitations, not, so to speak, the real thing.[3]

Evolutionism's hidden message is that primitive peoples *need* the
state. It is this self-satisfied teleology that modern scholarship has
completely discredited. Marshall Sahlins's *Stone Age Economics*
popularized the general anthropological discovery that hunter-
gatherers did not – and do not – need agriculture, let alone the
state.[4] Their 'domestic mode of production' required only a few
hours of formal labour each day, although considerably more was
spent in maintaining those wider regional contacts necessary as an
insurance system for ecologically difficult times. These people were
leisured and affluent. Many of them, notably the North American
Indians, 'knew about' agriculture, but chose not to adopt it on a
full-time basis – not surprisingly, since it would have diminished
their leisure and reduced them to a life of toil. However, some
hunter-gatherers did adopt more settled agricultural practices,
perhaps being forced to do so by their failure to control population,
something which is a prerequisite for hunter-gatherer existence.[5]
But there is no complete correspondence between the invention or
adoption of agriculture and the origin of the state: primitive
agriculturalists abound, while early states do not.[6] Yet may it not be
the case that what matters is some sort of incremental increase in
complexity? Certainly, there is a measure of truth to the liberal
paradigm in so far as it suggests that complexity will encourage
specialization. Specialization among hunter-gatherers is known,
most notably for dealing with other bands, and it is relatively
common, either for purposes of war or economic distribution,
among tribes.[7] This had led to the creation of evolutionary theories
of a straightforwardly functionalist kind according to which there is
a natural revolutionary progression from band to tribe, and then
from chiefdom to state.[8]

It is at this point that Marxism wreaks its revenge on the liberal
viewpoint. There is a great deal of evidence to show that primitive

peoples were at once prepared to allow for specialization *and* to resist any attempt to make it permanent. The most appealing example of a society acting against the exploitation which it knew settled state rule would bring is that provided by the fate of Geronimo. This famed Indian leader had been entrusted with the leadership of his tribe in order to avenge a particular wrong; once that had been done, the members of his tribe regularly refused to follow his ambitious designs – so much so that he was able to take only two braves on one war outing![9] Obviously, hunter-gatherers are so thin on the ground that they are scarcely the stuff on which states can be built. But state-builders had no more luck with tribesmen. Attempts at coercion were followed by evasion: nomads could disappear easily, while there was usually new land to which agriculturalists could turn. In all this, there is much evidence of a cyclical pattern: movement towards a state, in the form of more centralized chiefdoms of various types, is followed remorselessly by repeated retreat from it, perhaps especially once the implications of permanent rule are realized. The proper manner of conceptualizing the origins of the state forced upon us by these findings is obvious: the state is unnatural, and an explanation of its origins requires us to specify why it was that human beings, so good at evasion hitherto, suddenly became caught inside permanent organizations of co-ercion. What social process resulted in the circumscription of social activities, and the consequent 'caging' of human beings in states?

Answers to this conundrum have fallen into two categories. The first is essentially ecological in character. It makes much of a connection between alluvial agriculture and the rise of the state. The importance of this connection is simple. Irrigation works – and date and olive trees – tie agricultural producers very firmly to the land, and thus make them better fodder for states; being so tied makes it harder, in other words, to escape caging. The most subtle account which has noticed this connection sees the early state very much as the result of an unconscious flipping motion from functionalism to exploitation. A chiefdom in a river valley would have to undertake so many roles – most notably helping in trade, irrigation and storage – that eventually it would be able to move from the provision of services to the creation of central place coercion.[10]

The second strand of recent scholarship has stressed the religious origins of the state. The background assumption in this case is that the breakthrough to the state was a very major matter indeed. It went so much against the grain, it is claimed, that it was only made possible by the fact that coercion was accepted because it was, at least initially, in the service of the divine.[11] Put so simply, this argument does not have a great deal of force. For there were many chiefdoms, for example, those of Wessex and Polynesia, in which specialized ritual services were performed without full caging into states taking place. But it is possible to specify this religious element in such a way that it becomes a necessary part of any account of the origins of the state; in this matter we can do no better than follow Patricia Crone's analysis of 'The Tribe and the State'. Her argument stresses the sea change in human affairs that the acceptance of state organizations represents: a tribe is a commonsensical notion, being a political community based upon kinship; in contrast, a state is very different since it seeks to organize people by means of concepts which are not familiar from personal experience at all. Hence, on a priori grounds, it is indeed likely that a state could only be formed by recourse to demands believed to be supernatural. The historical evidence about Mesopotamia supports this view: the earliest form of the state was that of the temple economy, the principal purpose of which was to feed the gods. Importantly, there is no great evidence of social inegalitarianism at this time, although social division *followed* the creation of the state; what is striking instead is the fact that all humans were held to be inferior to the gods. But the situation in Mesopotamia differed from that in Polynesia – made much of by modern evolutionists like Sahlins and Service as a place in which tribal organization was supposedly likely to have led, but for the impact of the West, to pristine state formation – in two ways:

> Whether states would or would not have developed on their own, however, the dynamic potential of the Polynesian chiefdoms did not lie in the local version of tribal organisation . . . but . . . in religion. Had the Polynesian gods been more demanding, temple-building might well have generated new social and political roles here as it did in Sumeria; but for one reason or another they were too complacent. One suspects that they were too complacent precisely *because* a perfectly satisfactory tribal system existed; differently put, one suspects that state structures emerged among the Sumerians all the more easily in that no tribal organisation had been developed.[12]

A little Kierkegaardian 'fear and trembling' seems, in this view, necessary to a real religion: a divinity should not appease! Equally important, however, is the absence of tribal organization that allowed the caging of human beings in permanent states.

These accounts are not at odds with each other; rather they accentuate different elements of a single process, and illuminate each other at the same time. Thus ecological caging helps explain the loss of tribal ties. Is it not likely that the harshness of the conception of the divine was itself related to that loss? None the less, it is important to reiterate that we do not, and probably never will, have a unified general theory of the origins of pristine states; there are simply too few cases to allow this. Moreover, not all such states were born in alluvial river valleys, and ecological caging cannot in consequence account for the notably harsh gods of Meso-America. We simply do not have enough evidence to know whether this makes the general account of the origins of states offered here invalid or not.

If it is difficult to explain satisfactorily the emergence of the pristine state, it is not in the least hard to explain the creation of secondary states. Traditional explanations of the origins of the state seem so plausible to us because the factors they identify *do* play important roles in the creation of secondary states.[13] Thus it was not at all long before the first and tiny Mesopotamian state found that centralized control had enormous military benefits. By perhaps 2300 BC, Sargon of Akkad was turning this military capacity towards the creation of the first imperial system. Thereafter the pages of ancient history are populated with militarily created states – from the Hittites to the Persians, from the Assyrians to the Macedonians – which rise and fall with ponderous regularity. All this can be put very simply. Once the state was invented, its capacities for organizing military power meant that there was no going back to arcadian bliss.[14]

This suggests an important conclusion about the nature of social evolution, and it is one which lies at the back of our minds in this book. The fact that most evolutionary theories have been, so to speak, naive and automatic – the mere placing of one stage on top of another without offering much idea as to mechanisms accounting for transitions between them – does not mean that we can do without the concept of evolution altogether. Certain basic changes in historical means of social organization have changed the terms according to which all societies must operate, and these changes deserve to be called 'evolutionary'. But the best theory of social evolution available is neo-episodic. There is no teleology inherent to the historical process guaranteeing inevitable progress; the breakthroughs which matter tend to be the result of fortuitous openings rather than the result of some inexorable logic.[15] Most social organizations try to adapt to their circumstances, to achieve an equilibrium with them; fundamental social change tends, therefore, to be something which positively goes against the grain of social actors and their organizations. The makers of fundamental social change are best conceptualized as adaptive *failures*. This certainly helps us to make sense of the people who were forced to adopt agriculture and to those who eventually became caged in states. This notion will prove equally helpful in making sense of the rise of the West, to which we can now turn.

The European Dynamic

This chapter is concerned with an evolutionary breakthrough as important as the very invention of the state. It explains the emergence, in one part of the world at a particular point in time, of the modern state and of modern capitalism. Our claim will be that these emerged in tandem in a complicated process of interaction; this process is illuminated by the comparative method. We begin by outlining the socioeconomic baselines that limited state capacity in the agrarian world, and then describe the successful adaptation that oriental civilizations made to these circumstances. This background makes it possible to understand the 'adaptive failure' of Europe, doomed to dynamism because it was unable to establish equilibrium.

Puny leviathans

If the invention of the state changed the pattern of history, it remains very important to stress that early states had nothing like the real powers of the states of our own world. It is easy to demonstrate the fundamental weakness of early agrarian states. This weakness had its roots in the limitations of transportation and communication, the scarcity of resources, and the absence of a political or social infrastructure able to facilitate the raising of revenue and the mobilization of the people. These problems fed into each other. The scarcity of resources meant that rulers found it difficult to organize and maintain the personnel needed for population counts, land surveys, and other types of inspection necessary for the regular assessment of taxes. Under conditions such as these, corruption was common and taxation was a difficult and sporadic task. The cost of raising money was high in comparison

with the modern era, and this limited the size and regula
revenue. Primitive means of transportation and communic
limits on the movement toward economic or cultural integr
Large territories could be conquered and ostensibly be plac
under the control of a ruler, but peasants and villagers would have
little to do with the larger political entity. The vast majority
continued to live in more or less self-sufficient villages with more or
less autonomous cultures of their own, a fact which rendered the
political unity of pre-industrial societies precarious. Primitive
means of transportation and communication also meant that
information was continuously in short supply and that the dispatch
of advisers, troops, and other personnel – all the stuff of territorial
rule – was a very laboured process. It was impossible in the agrarian
era, at least in a land-based area, genuinely to mobilize social
forces, given that a bullock pulling a cart of grain would eat its load
within a hundred miles. This sort of logistical problem accounts for
the fact that the actual military striking range of ancient armies was
far less, as Donald Engel has demonstrated in a brilliant intellectual
exercise, than their ideologists claimed – and less, too, than most
historians have believed.[1] The high levels of formal despotism of
early states were matched by insignificant infrastructural capacities;
such states were but puny leviathans.

The minimal nature of the pre-industrial state meant that a wide
variety of autonomous groups and associations managed most
social and political tasks. Such 'self-help' groups were, in the first
instance, primarily kinship groups. The prospects were often bleak
for individuals unattached to such kinship groups, although in some
areas guilds, sectarian organizations, religious groups and other
voluntary associations could serve as kinship's organizational
equivalent. In general, states thus sat on top of social relationships
they could not control and did little to alter.[2]

Orientalism as a norm

Oriental civilizations adapted successfully to these socioeconomic
constraints. This is not to deny the huge amount of sound and fury in
the history of such civilizations. None the less, this does not detract
from the systemic nature of stability: dynasties came and went, but
structures remained the same. In this section, the nature of these
successful adaptions is described. Emphasis is placed on the ways in
which intellectuals combined, as bureaucrats or as specialists in

religious meaning, with their social formations so as to produce highly different state–society relations. Despite diversity, oriental civilizations were similar in having states with strong despotic and weak infrastructural powers; they tended, accordingly, to affect economic life in the same way. A warning must be issued at this point. It is not the case that the social system of each civilization that we consider was, but for political blockages, equally ready for capitalist development. The human *matériel*, or the productive forces were, as Smith and Marx respectively stressed, more advanced in Europe than elsewhere. The realization that the comparative account of this chapter cannot have the neatness of a laboratory experiment necessitates specifying the claims to be made. In the West, a particular type of state was a necessary but not a sufficient condition for the rise of capitalism. Similarly, our thesis about oriental civilizations must sometimes be that capitalist forces, had they been present, would have been blocked by the political system.

Imperial China

The Chinese empire was bounded to the north by the Great Wall, which was manned by troops whose supplies came to be sent up the Grand Canal from the fertile, double-cropping rice lands of the south. What is implied by this simple statement? The extensive area of the empire was created and held together by military might; the reach of culture was thus less than that of military might.[3] The examination system which encouraged intellectuals to serve this civilization as bureaucrats (the mandarins) rather than as priests was created by the state, first under the Han and, much more decisively, under the Tang. Does the presence of an imperial state manned by bureaucrats schooled in a statist creed give evidence of a genuine leviathan, a really strong state within the agrarian world?

There were never enough mandarins to form an efficient governing class. The first Ming emperor in 1371 sought to have as few as 5488 mandarins in government service, and by the sixteenth century there were still only about 20,400 in the empire as a whole, plus another 50,000 minor officials.[4] A local official might well have managed 500–1000 square miles with the aid of only three assistants. So the Chinese state did not have the means of total control envisaged in Wittfogel's fantasy of *Oriental Despotism*.[5] Most social norms were created and enforced by a kinship system which, luckily, was not often turned against the state. Of course, the state sought to gain autonomy from society, but arbitrary action against individuals was counterbalanced by an inability of the state fundamentally to go against the gentry class as a whole. The state sought to improve the economy but had very limited means with which to push through any plan of its own. Reformer after reformer tried to establish a decent land registry as the basis for a proper taxation system, but all were defeated by the refusal of landlords to co-operate. The empire as a whole witnessed a power stand-off between state and society which led to the inability to generate a large total sum of societal energy.

This stalemate can be seen at work in 'the dynastic cycle'. A newly established dynasty sought to create a healthy peasant base both for its tax and military potential. Yet even without internal or external pressures, the state tended to lose control of society. The local power of the gentry enabled them to increase their estates and to avoid taxation. Other pressures on the empire were usually present as well. Internally, an expansion of population, by no means discouraged by the gentry, eventually caused land hunger and peasant rebellions. Externally, the nomads on the borders found the empire more and more attractive as its prosperity waxed in front of their eyes. Such nomads were often employed as imperial mercenaries, and they thereby learnt military techniques which, when allied with the military resource inherent in their great mobility, made them a formidable force; the state was, in consequence, forced to increase taxation rates. It was at this moment that the power stand-off between state and society proved to be important: landlords chose to shelter peasants who refused to pay such increased taxation, and thereby increased their own local power. The combination of feudal disintegration and over-population led to a constant decrease in the number of taxpaying peasant smallholders. Rodinski cites the census of 754 AD which showed that there were only 7.6 million taxpayers out of a total population of 52.8 million.[6] In such circumstances the state was forced to tax even more heavily where it could and this in turn fuelled peasant unrest. Breakdown ensued.

None the less, the Chinese empire was restored time and time again. The mandarins, unlike the Latin Christian Church at the fall of Rome, remained true to the imperial deal. On a number of occasions barbarians tried to rule without them, partly because the mandarins were wont to stay away from a dynasty that did not respect the fundamentals of Confucianism. Any consideration of the rather small numbers of the elite shows that an enormous confidence trick was played on the gentry. They remained loyal to the state, but the paucity of their numbers is evidence that they did not do all that well from it. The argument being made is that there was a definite autonomy of the state, of the political, in Chinese history because the state was strong enough to force class relations into this particular pattern. This makes us consider the key question: in what ways, if any, did the imperial form affect the Chinese economy?

Medieval China did witness considerable economic advance of a broadly capitalist type. Interestingly, the greatest expansion took place during a period of *disunity*. The northern Sung ruled China from 960 until 1127, but even they were faced with the militant, nomadic Jurchen. Disunity encouraged the southern Sung to build a navy in order to man all waterways which stood between them and their northern competitors. More generally, the markets and cities gained autonomy during this period of disunity in Chinese history. The quality of coinage provided by states tended to improve during disunity because traders would not themselves return to or trust governments which manipulated the coinage.[7] But how did the empire, when it was reunited, react to capitalist forces that had flourished previously? The state limited the autonomy that cities had gained. Little is known about the collapse of the iron and steel industries of Sung China. However, we can explain the collapse of Sung naval strength. The foundation of a native dynasty which improved the Grand Canal undermined the navy; most obviously, between 1371 and 1567, all foreign trade was banned. The most spectacular way in which politics could affect the economy concerned the fate of the explorations undertaken by the eunuch admiral Cheng-Ho in the 1430s. The mandarins were always extremely jealous of the emergence of sources of power alternative to their own. They were naturally opposed to Cheng-Ho precisely because he was a eunuch, whose cause was promoted by the eunuchs at court. Thus the centralization of political life mattered. Although the bureaucracy was not able to penetrate far into society, it could and did prevent other forces from gaining much autonomy. An earlier classic instance of this had been the suppression of Buddhist monasteries.

Chinese imperial government deserves the appellation *capstone*. The Chinese elite shared a culture, and sat atop a series of separate 'societies' which it did not wish to penetrate or mobilize; it feared that horizontal linkages, whether religious or economic in character, that it could not see would get out of control. This capstone government blocked the fully-fledged emergence of intensive capitalist relationships. The concern of the mandarinate was less with intensifying social relationships than in seeking to prevent any linkages which might diminish its power. This is *not* to say that the impact of the state upon capitalism must always, as naive liberals claim, be negative. A different type of state, the European organic state, was, we shall see, capable, once market relationships were established, of providing crucial services for capitalism. The Chinese state was incapable of so doing:

> It must be pointed out that in the late Ming most of the service facilities indispensable to the development of capitalism were clearly lacking. There was no legal protection for the businessman, money was scarce, interest rates high and banking undeveloped. . . . At the same time merchants and entrepreneurs were hindered by the frequent roadblocks on the trade routes, government purchase orders and forced contributions, the government's near monopoly of the Grand Canal and active involvement in manufacturing. On the other hand, the security and status of land ownership, the tax-exemption enjoyed by those who purchased official rank, and the non-progressive nature of the land tax increased the attractions of farming to the detriment of business involvement.[8]

Politics and culture in China tended to have the same extensive reach, and this pattern was crucial to China's fate. Centralized power allowed for the blocking of capitalism while the absence of any real competitors made this sort of low-intensity rule a viable proposition. The three remaining world civilizations considered in this chapter also had extensive reach. But they differ in having, for crucial periods, cultures more extensive than polities. In all these three cases social identity was achieved and maintained without the benefit of state regulation: ideology created and did not reflect a society.[9] The absence of a single political centre suggests that capitalism might well prosper, free from bureaucratic interference. This was a vital factor in the rise of the West, but its exact nature can only be understood if India and Islam are considered first. They demonstrate that the absence of an empire was not enough in itself to ensure the triumph of capitalism. Fragmentation was but one of the factors in the political package that allowed and abetted nascent capitalism.

The Land of the Brahmans

The *Rig-Veda* makes it clear that Aryan invaders were not able to rest easily in the land they had invaded. Warfare with the native population, possibly different in colour, was continuous. This situation contrasts with those that faced nomad invaders elsewhere. Those who invaded the Roman Empire rapidly bowed before Christian monotheism, as might be expected since most nomads are absorbed into the larger worlds they conquer. The Islamic nomad conquerors of the Middle East were completely different in having their own monotheistic religion, which made them feel superior: they were not absorbed by a civilization but rather created their own. Perhaps the situation of the Aryan invaders lay between these extreme positions: 'they accommodated themselves to a life which allowed a certain separateness together with a certain independence'.[10] This is to offer the beginnings of an explanation of caste. It is necessary to say something about the origins of this extraordinary system if we are to understand the character of state–society relations in this civilization.

In China, intellectuals, at the behest of the state, produced a type of Caesaropapist doctrine, and such fusion of religious and political power occurred elsewhere. In India, a *division* took place between secular and religious power from very early times. But ideas do not always translate into reality. The Brahmans' claim to speak for the social order was attacked by the Nandas and Mauryans who united India under a single imperial umbrella. Interesting efforts were made to produce an ethic suited to the empire as a whole. The emperor Asoka introduced and generalized the ideas of *dhamma* which stressed, as did Confucianism, social responsibility and service to the state. The imperial drive tried to create loyalty to the emperor rather than to the social order. Power and hierarchy were to be reconciled, and the emperor, as the fount of law, was to become leader of the community. An elective affinity was established between this political threat and the religious threat to Brahmanical control represented by Buddhism. Asoka became a Buddhist. It seems likely that he hoped that the universalism of a salvationist ethic would combine with the universal political order of the empire.

The elective affinity between Buddhism and empire never gelled sufficiently to create a stable imperial system. But why, at some later date, was the creation of a universal empire, backed by

Buddhism, not achieved? Perhaps Buddihsm did *not* fit neatly with the rule of emperors and kings. Rulers may have become suspicious of Buddhism's relation to the political realm on account of the vast wealth acquired by Buddhist monasteries. A further reason for the failure of Buddhism to triumph over its rivals lay in its concentration on salvation. Buddhism simply turned its back on the social, Durkheimian aspect of religion: it offered no real guidance, until the modern period, for as basic a social need as the regulation of marriage! In contrast, the greatest achievement of neo-Brahmanism lay in its capacity to organize social relationships. The Brahmans responded to the challenges of empire and Buddhism by extending and regularizing the services they performed on every occasion of the life cycle, and their presence became firmly anchored in the locality. The *Laws of Manu* show Brahmans providing laws to organize every aspect of social life. The Brahman-dominated social order did the work of an empire not just in opening up new lands but in the most fundamental way of all: in bringing peace and social order. Its achievements were real and significant, and it is not surprising that the Brahman came to occupy so high a place in Indian civilization.

Brahmanical organization of society distanced itself from both wealth and power. This withdrawal affected political life very markedly. Kings were recognized as individuals rather than as representatives of longer-lasting states, and few expectations were held of them. Their duty in life was simply to fight, and they had no other secular duty than that of protecting the social order: the state was *custodial*. Politics had very shallow roots in society. Kings could not gain regular taxation, but were offered tribute on an irregular basis. This was the cause of constant instability of political rule in traditional India.[11]

This form of state–society relations was unhelpful for economic life in two ways. First, caste proved debilitating to economic life because of its hierarchical conception of social life. Trade expanded during the Gupta period, but so too did caste regulations, and these made its salience more limited. Further, caste did not allow for a flexible division of labour.[12] This divisiveness of caste played a deleterious role as far as the advance of knowledge was concerned. The great advances made by the Brahmans in mathematics and astronomy were treated as their secret knowledge; obstacles were placed in the way of the diffusion of such knowledge. The point being made deserves emphasis. There is a great difference between

Hinduism, on the one hand, and Islam and Christianity, on the other. Our modern social science notion of society implicitly contains conceptions of universality and reciprocity. The sense of community created by Islam and Christianity was one in which, at least in principle, all human beings could participate. Fundamental spiritual equality was written into the society by the promise of salvation held out to everyone. Indian society was not universalist in this sense. It had no sense of universal brotherhood. Its society was a community based on division rather than the possibility of shared experience. This must have had adverse effects on the intensity of social, and therefore economic, interaction. It is very important to note that all this amounts to saying that Indian society would very probably not have witnessed economic advance of a capitalist type *whatever its political constitution had been*. Perhaps we should not exaggerate this: there was always more flexibility to the system than is often allowed, and there is also some evidence of the political system serving as an *impediment* to economic forces whose character seems to have been capitalist. Brahmanical organization of social life by means of caste created unstable polities. Instability made for predatory rule. Kings had power for such a short period that they simply took what they could: as the state was not long-lasting, there could be no conception of nurturing merchant activities with a view to long-term tax revenue. Grants to temples could not be touched by kings, and the temples consequently grew incredibly rich.[13] When states changed hands, so too did landowner-ship and tax farming rights. This discouraged investment in the land which was to be exploited as much as possible while it was possessed – a situation in which peasants as well had no reason to invest. The economic cost of weak polities can be highlighted in a most dramatic way. It proved impossible to protect the north-west frontier, even though a Great Wall here would have been extremely effective; in consequence India suffered a whole series of invasions, some of them hugely destructive.

Islam and pastoralism

Hindu India stepped back from China in two ways: its extensive culture was not universal, while its states were transient, predatory and therefore completely incapable of providing social infrastruc-ture. Islam boasts a culture which is both extensive and highly universalistic, and this can be seen as an advance not only on the

Indian but also on the Chinese situation. But Islam had weak polities, resembling, albeit for different reasons, those of India, and in this matter it is less advanced than the admittedly weak Chinese political form. We can proceed by characterizing Islamic culture, seeing how this fitted with pastoralism so as to produce weak states, and then establishing how this pattern affected economic life.

A religious vision united the Arab tribes and thereby allowed them great military capacity. The Islamic conquerors, as noted, brought a monotheism with them; they possessed 'force *and* value'.[14] This inheritance presented problems when rule over conquered lands had to be consolidated and regulated. The Umayyads were able to rule for some time on the basis of traditional kinship cohesion, but such politics was far removed from original Islamic purposes. The Arabs did not 'feel at home' in their conquered lands. They were unable to integrate with the settled population; since they were the carriers of their own religious vision they scorned and did not wish to be absorbed by 'civilization'. Tribesmen had not bargained for, nor were they prepared to accede to, taxation, and they hankered for the simplicity and egalitarianism of that tribal life which had marked the earliest period of Islamic history. It is in these Umayyad years that the experts in the Word (the *ulama*) codified Islam. These intellectuals were not integrated into the first caliphate and the codification they made harked back to the simpler tribal past, a past in which there was little room for the necessities of power.[15] Mainstream Islam, in other words, came to have a distrust for the exercise of political power. Sharia law was neither a Caesaropapist doctrine supporting imperial power nor one like Christianity, which said that the purpose of religion was purely spiritual, and that accordingly power relations did not matter and could be left to proceed on their own course. Government thus had very slim roots in society, and stability came to depend upon such solidarity as the rulers of society – or the slaves they used – could achieve, as is true of most conquest societies. As such social solidarity tends to be evanescent, government in classical Islam tended to be highly unstable.

Possession of the sacred norms of society did not, however, enable the *ulama* to turn their backs on political power as had Indian intellectuals. The reason for this divergence lies in the nature of pastoralism. Power was needed because nomads were militarily powerful; Islamic civilization was not just made in the image of tribal simplicity, but also had to contend with the continuing presence of tribes. Pastoralism combined with the rigor of Islamic ideology in a manner first fully spelt out by Ibn Khaldun.[16]

Nomads are not completely independent. Ibn Khaldun noted that the city is necessary for them: certain craft work, such as tanning and heavier metalwork, requires static equipment which would *per se* invalidate nomad existence. But such material can be obtained by trading. A trading centre requires a government so that market transactions can be reliable and regular. In North Africa, government control is limited to the cities and their surroundings. The essential contrast, to use a Moroccan expression, is between the *bled el makhzen*, the area of order, and the *bled el siba*, the area of tribal dissidence. It should be noted that the third party, the peasantry – thin on the ground in North Africa but of great historical importance in Egypy, Iran, Iraq, Syria and Anatolia – plays no active role in this picture: tribes, rather than peasants, have military force. The dynamics of Ibn Khaldunian sociology result from the inability of cities to govern themselves. In European society such self-government ultimately depended upon the ability of cities to raise their own troops (or to purchase mercenaries) able to defeat organized armies operating over a relatively pacified terrain. Muslim society in the arid zone was not at all like this. Urban citizens faced a land of dissidence capable of great military surges. Those who could not defend themselves looked for a defender, and they found it in *one* tribe, capable of fighting off tribal incursions and of providing order for markets. But a tribe, as soon as it became the ruler of a city, automatically began to suffer degeneracy. The quality that had allowed the tribe to come to prominence in the first place was social solidarity, but the ease and luxury of city life undermined this. So, although citizens supported the tribal rulers at first, they would become restive, typically by about the third generation of the ruling dynasty. The *ulama* would begin by serving the ruling house as administrators and judges. Yet they possessed the sacred norms of Islam; these, because of their precise codification, were not nearly as much at the mercy of secular power as was the relatively spiritual doctrine of Christianity. Some *ulama* would become discontented with the ruling house as it became corrupt. In time, they would declare the ruling house to be impious, and invite in one of the tribes from the areas of dissidence. It is here that the presence of an ideology shared with the tribesmen matters. This manner of accession to power probably explains why Islamic culture, more extensive than any state, was maintained: a ruling house coming to power as the result of a religious spasm was unlikely to turn against Islam and never had the time to do so.

This Ibn Khaldunian circulation of elites suggests the term *cyclical* polity for the state in classical Islam. This polity was as transient as the custodial state of India, and its effects upon economic relationships were similar. The universalism of Islam did make this a great trading civilization, and there is sufficient evidence of market activity to make important the question of whether the political form proved an impediment.[17] Clearly, transient and predatory polities had debilitating effects upon economic life in general. Two types of landholding deserve special attention, the *iqta* and the *waqf*. The former of these were land-grants given to the supporters of the ruling dynasty. Crucially, as dynasties changed, so did the landholders. This partly explains the character of the *waqf*, formally a religious endowment and therefore typically not touched by a new ruling house, but often in fact a means whereby a family could draw a certain income from the land in covert form. This dual type of landholding proved inimical to agricultural advance. Insecurity of tenure encouraged predatory usage, and there was little genuine investment in the land. Equally importantly, Muslim society did not allow cities to be autonomous: the burgher was less important than the military governor.[18] The presence of government made political favours more important than the market.

In summary, the cyclical state in Islam was unstable, and this affected the economy in two ways. It was arbitrary and predatory enough to interfere directly in the market, with the workings of justice and the autonomy of cities. On the other hand, the government was weak. Land went out of circulation with a corresponding loss of tax revenue and a limitation upon the number of state servants it was possible to recruit. Few services could be provided by the state.

There is a puzzle about Islam. Both Islam and Christianity held together a large area in which equal citizens could recognize each other; both these civilizations centred themselves on a sense of community. Why then did not Islam similarly help capitalism? In Europe the ability of a merchant to move with his capital away from persecution was allied to the presence of a more organic type of state which was in place over long periods of time. This type of state was forced to provide infrastructural services for society, both because of the pre-existence of a civil society and because of the need to raise revenue to compete in war with other similarly stable states. In Islam, no such organic states existed. The fear of tribesmen meant that urban strata could not rule themselves and a premium was accordingly placed upon military power. Governments elsewhere were unlikely to be more stable, so that moving one's capital did not avoid predation. The explanation for the difference is military. In Europe the emergence of states forced the aristocracy to gain profits from land rather than from warfare, and the reasonably settled character of the core of Europe meant that monarchs had to turn to the provision of infrastructural services to gain revenue. In Muslim society, wars remained the greatest potential source of profit.[19] The whole point can be put in a nutshell. Muslim society did *not* have a multipolar state system equivalent to that of Europe in which rationalization by the states of their societies occurred under pressure of war. On the contrary, states came and went, and were of larger or smaller size at various periods; but they never lasted long enough ever to be rationalized at all.

The European exception

The central argument of this section is that the European state differed from those of the Orient in being despotically weak and, over time, infrastructurally strong. We will explain why this was possible, and how it affected and was affected by larger market society. We stress in particular that the socioeconomic dynamism that marked Europe's ascendency can be traced to a unique combination of cultural unity and political fragmentation. Let us consider both of these elements in turn.

Unity emerged slowly during the Middle Ages as Germanic invaders occupied the northern and western regions of the Roman Empire and came to embrace its Christian doctrines. Indeed, perhaps the most remarkable turning point in European history was that extraordinary *trahison des clercs* involved in the church's spurning of the Roman Empire. St Augustine's *City of God* famously argued that God's timetable was his own, and the Church in the West chose to take civilization to the barbarians rather than to wait for them, as had the Chinese mandarins, to convert to the imperial form. It was this betrayal, as much as any weaknesses of Roman political structures, which accounts for the failure to reconstitute classical civilization. None the less, the Christian Church was, to use Thomas Hobbes's phrase, the 'ghost of the Holy

Roman empire', and it did much of the extensive work previously accomplished by the legions. If the political structure of the Roman Empire was swept away, a core of law and culture remained and was built upon by the Church. This common culture had important implications for economic and political innovation. The sense of community it established helped to create a consensus within which contractual relationships could work: the extensive work of the church facilitated, in other words, the emergence of intensive economic relations within a large European market as early as 1000.[20] Cultural homogeneity also led in time to the relatively easy diffusion of organizational innovations, the expansion of territorial control of the state, and the movement of administrative personnel.[21]

The cultural unity of medieval Europe was matched by its political fragmentation. It is important that the Germanic invasions of the region took place in many waves and over many centuries. This ensured territorial diversity in the locations of political power. The feudal patterns of social and economic organization also served to disperse power and privatize property rights across the region. Political power was located in the manors of rural lords. Cities were left uncommanded by more overarching political authorities and became centres of trade and non-agricultural production. The fragmentation of political power was not beyond challenge and European history records various attempts to develop an imperial structure after the fall of Rome. The Church sought on occasion to establish a theocratic empire. But its attempts always failed because it never possessed its own army capable of disciplining a jumble of competing states. But how did those states come into being in the first place? As we have noted, the fact that *several* sets of barbarians came into Europe at the end of the Roman Empire doubtless was an initial condition in favour of a multipolar system. But we can add to this that the church played a very notable role in making a secular empire impossible. Most obviously, it welcomed the rise of states which were able to give more secure protection to its own property. But there is a more important point to be made: the Church refused to serve as second fiddle in an empire equivalent to those of China and Byzantium, and thus did not create a Caesaropapist doctrine in which a single emperor was elevated to semi-divine status. Rather, the Church's habitual playing of power politics encouraged the formation of separate states, with balance of power politics always ensuring that no single one become dominant. And this was not the only way in which Christianity provided the best shell for the emergence of states. The Church provided the numinous aspects of kingship – most notably, the coronation and the singing of the *Laudes Irae* – that made a king more than one among equals. Even more importantly, the Church attacked extended kinship systems.[22] In the other world civilizations the lower classes could often rely on kinship systems as a means of protection and mutual aid. The removal of this weapon of the lower classes made the European peasant that much better fodder for state formation. This combination of diversity within unity affected development in three ways.

A counter-factual proposition

Imagine what European history might have been like had the Roman Empire somehow been reconstituted, or had any empire taken its place. We have seen that the Chinese empire was too centralized for its logistical capacity, and thus tended to produce capstone government based on the accurate perception that secondary organizations were dangerous. Empires usually sought to encourage the economy, but this form of government never ultimately allowed the Chinese economy sufficient leeway to gather self-sustaining momentum. Why should an imperial Europe have been any different?

This counter-factual proposition can be put in a rather different manner. All historians agree that Max Weber was indeed correct in the more materialistic part of his theory concerning the rise of the West, namely in his contention that only in Europe did cities gain full autonomy, possessing their own governments and armies rather than being controlled by the arbitrary rule of others. These city states provided a space in which the merchant was king, and in which bourgeois values could gel and solidify.[23] These city states recovered the culture of the classical world, and this ideological legacy proved important both in the establishment of national states at the time of the Reformation and in the creation of the nation state by the French revolutionaries. We live in the world created by this civilization. Why was there such autonomy? The northern Italian cities gained autonomy because there was no single centre of power in Europe. Specifically, they benefited from being in a power vacuum between pope and emperor, such that they were able to get the best for themselves by opportunistically chopping and changing their allegiance.[24] How much they owed to their ability to experiment is simply seen: once they became part of the Spanish mini-empire they contributed virtually nothing new to European civilization. And much the same point could be made by indulging in a 'thought experiment'. Had Philip II created a long-lasting empire based on his new Spanish possessions, what would have happened to the social experiments taking place in the Netherlands and Great Britain? It seems likely that social innovation at the peripheries would have been ruled out by any imperial consolidation.

The organic state

This first point amounts to reiterating that political fragmentation was a necessary condition for the autonomy of the market. But the Indian and Islamic cases have demonstrated that such fragmentation is not sufficient by itself to encourage economic dynamism. What else was involved? It might at first sight seem contradictory to say that the organic state helped economic development after the largely negative comments made up to now about state interference. But there are *different* types of state in different historical and social circumstances. Two general principles about the relations of government to the economy can be maintained. First, the absence of all government is disastrous since it encourages disorder and localism, and thus prevents trade. The insistence that Christianity held Europe together shows that no anarchist vision is encouraged here. Second, bureaucratic and predatory governments were indeed hostile to economic development. As noted, it is mistaken to consider such government strong since it was based on weak infrastructural penetration of the society; indeed its arbitrariness results, in part, from that weakness. This gives us the clue to the distinctiveness of the European state: a limit to arbitrariness combined with – indeed, in part caused – considerable and ever-increasing infrastructural penetration.

The limitations on the despotic power and the simultaneous encouragement of intrastructural power were the result of major constraints on the state. In the first place, the European state evolved slowly and doggedly in the midst of pre-existing social relationships. One uniqueness of the West is the role that parliaments and other deliberative assemblies played in its history: indeed so unique has this role been that German historians have considered the *Standesstaat* – the representation of the three functional estates of Church, nobility and city – a distinctive stage in world history. It is quite clear that the prominence of such assemblies owes a great deal to the Church. Since it owned so much land it was as jealous as any noble of the powers of the crown to tax. Hence it generalized two tags of Canon law – 'no taxation without representation' and 'what touches all must be approved by all', – which became crucial to these estates. But 'liberties' were widely diffused throughout society, and churchmen had allies among nobles, burghers and yeomen. This deserves to be called a civil society. The building of strong royal power required that monarchs came to terms with this society, and across Europe distinctive patterns of co-optation and subordination of these representative institutions emerged. In England the parliaments survived the challenges from the Tudors and the Stuarts. In France and Prussia, the monarchy was able to undermine the various assemblies, but only after considerable effort and through the building of a large administrative apparatus. In Spain, the monarchy and the Cortes were left without a clear resolution. This historical reworking of the relations between the crown and civil society, which occupied the efforts of European elites for much of the seventeenth century, was crucial in laying the foundation of the social and political infrastructure of the modern nation state.[25]

The paradox of this situation is that restraint on government in the end generated a larger sum of power in society. Perhaps the most important mechanism in this process was the making of money via the provision of a certain infrastructure to the society. This is most clearly seen in the provision of justice. Fees were charged for every legal transaction, and these came to provide an important part of the revenue of most monarchs after about 1200. This is not to say that the law was equally open for all to use; but it *was* available. This mattered.

European states provided other sorts of infrastructural help as well. They became good at managing disasters of various sorts; by the eighteenth century, for example, considerable help was available to the victims of earthquakes, while disease was quite rigidly controlled by quarantine laws.[26] Furthermore, the internal colonialism whereby the Scots, Irish and Welsh were integrated into a single community – a process repeated elsewhere in Europe – created a single market. In the more advanced European states this process went hand in hand with the removal of internal tariff barriers, and this was an incentive to trade. These policies were not designed with the improvement of the economy in view, but rulers *had* consciously

encouraged trade for a long time. They did so because a dispropor-
tionate bulk of their revenues came from customs and excise. They
sought to attract traders; a typical piece of legislation in this matter
being Edward I's *Carta Mercatoria* of 1297. And what is apparent is
that large sections of the powerful were prepared to give quite high
taxation revenues to the crown because they realized that their own
interests were usually being served. Tocqueville was right to note
that the English aristocracy and gentry manned local government
and taxed itself. The level of infrastructural support and penetration was correspondingly high. A Confucian bureaucrat who moved
every three years simply could not know enough about local
conditions to serve a particular area well. Representation to a
central assembly by local aristocrats created a different result.

The multipolar system of states

The complete 'formula' of the European dynamic is that competition between strong states inside a larger culture encouraged
the triumph of capitalism. Individual states did not exist in a
vacuum. They were rather part of a competing state system, and it
was that system, particularly the military organization it engen-
dered, that played a considerable part in determining the character
of individual states. Why was this?

A state system leads to a high degree of emulation. Early modern
Europe was marked by a group of states in close proximity and in
constant geopolitical and economic competition. When one state
found success in a particular form of economic or military organization and strengthened its international competitive advantage,
other states felt compelled to follow. The competitive system
provided incentives for states to attend to the efficient organization
of their economy and society; the common cultural system within
which the European states emerged allowed the innovations that
followed to be diffused with relative ease.[27] This emulation can be
very clearly seen in artistic matters, but it extended to the
establishment of various scientific clubs in eighteenth-century
France in conscious imitation of their English rivals. Such emulation is ultimately only possible between states which reocognized
each other as of more or less similar standing; empires do not tend
to copy the culture of small neighbours – mere barbarians!

The competitive processes inherent in the state system encouraged changes that were beneficial for economic growth. In the first

place, a state system always had an in-built escape system. This is most obviously true in human matters. The expulsion of the Jews from Spain and the Huguenots from France benefited, and was seen to benefit, other countries, and this served in the long run as a limitation on arbitrary government. Capital was equally mobile. State elites could not simply assume that capitalists within their territorial boundaries would provide the resources and revenues necessary for the military campaigns on the continent. In a recent essay, Charles Tilly has sketched these relationships between warmaking, capital accumulation, extraction, and European state-making. Tilly notes that leaders of nascent states, engaged in war with adjacent powerholders, needed to extract resources from local producers and traders. 'The quest inevitably involved them in establishing regular access to capitalists who could supply and arrange credit, and in imposing one form of regular taxation or another on the people and activities within their sphere of control.'[28] But capitalists were capable of movement, and therefore state officials had incentives to form alliances with various social classes and to foster capital accumulation.[29] At the earliest moment of European state-building, state elites were confronted with a double-edged imperative: to harness domestic wealth so as to strengthen the state's foreign position, but to do so in a way that would not scare off capitalists or diminish economic growth.[30] It was dangerous to ignore these rules. Thus Philip II's abuse of Antwerp led within a matter of years rather than decades to the rise of Amsterdam. In a brilliant passage making this point, William McNeill has shown that time and time again Philip II *wanted* to behave like an autocrat but the mobility of capital defeated him.[31] This was particularly true of his relationship with Liège, the foremost cannon producer of late sixteenth-century Europe. When Phillip pressurized them too hard, artisans and capitalists simply went elsewhere. A certain measure of decent and regularized behaviour was ensured by these means.

Perhaps the fundamental mechanism at work was that of military competition. Geopolitical competition induced states to copy the organizational arrangements of leading states. In the early modern period, the development of new and more efficient military organizations and systems of taxation to support large standing armies in France, Austria and the United Provinces led neighbouring states to incorporate these innovations.[32] State competition had beneficial economic consequences beyond the rationalization of fiscal and administrative structures, although these consequences were unintended. In Germany, dramatic defeat by Napoleon was ascribed to the impact of an ideologically motivated citizen army. The reform group around Hardenburg (including Scharnhorst and Gneisenau, and with Clausewitz as its greatest intellectual figure) realized that serfs could not provide such an army; the reforms of 1807, 1811 and 1818 changed the Prussian social structure at a stroke. The purpose of such changes was military but the commercialization of agriculture that resulted was economically beneficial.

As noted, the European state became able to generate far more power than its imperial rivals: thus the France of Louis XIV probably had as large an army as Ming China even though her population was 20 million rather than 150 million. This raises an important question. The organic quality of the European state arose from its having to accept and co-operate with other elements in civil society. Why was it, however, that the more powerful European state did not turn inwards in order to establish something more like an imperial system? Roughly speaking, the absolutist state tried precisely this, and it is important to reiterate how unsuccessful it was. It is conventional to compare the absolutist state of France with the constitutionalist state of Great Britain in order to give the impression of greater strength in the former case. This is, as noted, mistaken. The English system generated more power without an absolutist façade; it proved this in defeating France in war on every occasion except one in which the two countries met in the eighteenth century. It is hugely significant that by the middle of the eighteenth century France was sending its intellectuals to England, and was in other ways trying to copy English secrets. All this suggests that there must be a prime mover among the states in order to get competition to work in the first place. In fact, there were several prime movers in European history, the torch of progress being passed from Italy, to Holland and on to England. England played a highly significant part as such a torch-bearer, and it seems no accident that this state possessed a powerful and, crucially, centralized estates system, the presence of which, in combination with naval military strength which was useless for internal repression, probably explains why the absolutist path was avoided.

Conclusion

Let us summarize the argument. For market relationships to gain autonomy, extensive social interaction networks are needed. In China, such extensive networks were provided by the polity. However, imperial rule was, perhaps could only be, based upon the negative tactic of preventing horizontal linkages that it could not control; such bureaucratic interference eventually proved deleterious for the economy. In the non-imperial civilizations, extensive networks were guaranteed by ideological organizations without the presence of a central polity. But in both India and Islam the state was weak, and had no more capacity to penetrate and organize social relationships than had the Chinese imperial state. In addition, in India and Islam the state was short-lived, and thus predatory, and this accounts for the negative effect on economic relationships, although both societies, especially India, probably did not have powerful market forces at work in any case. Only when long-lasting states were forced by military competition to interact strongly with their civil societies was economic progress possible. It was, of course, virtually *miraculous* that economic progress and liberal political rule went hand in hand, that commerce had an elective affinity with liberty. That this was so represents a certain vindication for liberal social theory. But it must be remembered that this development would not have taken place without the framework of order and the infrastructural services provided nationally by a rather active state and internationally as the result of the normative integration established by the Latin Christian Church. The state mattered, *pace* Marxism, since productive forces needed a particular shell, at once restrained and supportive.

To speak of progress suggests a naive and offensive Eurocentrism. Hence, it should be stressed that the rise of the West was no more the result of a predetermined pattern than had been the creation of the pristine state. This breakthrough also resulted from failure – the inability to maintain the civilization of the Mediterranean in its classical form. The weakest link in the chain, to use Trotsky's expression, allowed for fundamental change. The breakthrough, of course, had enormous consequences, but it was itself fortuitous. Here again is evidence for the neo-episodic theory of social evolution which we favour.

The European Disaster

An institutional package can be good for one set of circumstances, but disastrous in others. Such seems to have been the case with the relations between states and capitalism. In the last chapter, we outlined the dynamic and progressive nature of that combination in early modern Europe. In this chapter, our concern is with the long European civil war that debilitated Europe between 1914 and 1945 and led to it losing its leading role; this long war resembled the Peloponnesion wars of classical Greece in that they changed the shape of world history. The combination that had been dynamic proved, once industry was applied to war, to be catastrophic.

Obviously, the fact that this was so has completely disrupted liberalism's hopes that the spread of commerce would bring with it peace and parliamentary rule. But we need to examine in detail the origins of the two world wars. More particularly, does the combination of states and *industrial* capitalism in and of itself, as realists believe, account for the European débâcle? An alternative explanation, most prominent in Marxism, wishes to draw attention to the societal impact of classes upon states. We begin with an examination of working classes, and then turn to the relations of capitalists with their states at the end of nineteenth century. We ask throughout the chapter about the impact of liberal political regimes. Did liberal regimes encourage peace, and would an extension of the liberal principle have ensured it? The record of liberalism as a whole will prove to be mixed, as is most clearly evident in the last section of this chapter dealing with the reaction of liberal states to the great revolutionary forces of Bolshevism and fascism, both spawned by defeat in the First World War, which came to dreadful prominence in the inter-war years.

Workers and states

Before 1914, there was a marked diversity in the way in which different nation states dealt with their working classes. Several variables explain this diversity. The style of working-class politics varies according to patterns of industrialization, with working classes that have been created during industrialization, as was that of Sweden, proving later to be good material for a corporatist style of political economy. Equally important is whether different conflicts are superimposed on top of each other.[1] A striking example of this was the superimposition of religious division on top of class conflict in late nineteenth-century France: this situation made it necessary for someone on the left to be at once anti-clerical and socialist. This naturally exacerbated the intensity of political conflict. It stands in decided contrast to the British case in which a religion, Methodism, was available for workers; it has long been believed that this diminished the intensity of class conflict in nineteenth-century Britain.[2] However, it is a third variable – the organization of the state and the policies it adopted – that is by far the most important:

> . . . the major determinant of the forms of political action adopted by the different national labour movements was the role of the state and of the social groups it claimed to represent; for at the level of industrial action clear similarities existed between similar occupations in different countries. Furthermore, it remains true that certain kinds of government interference in industrial relations did transform what began as economic protest into political action.[3]

Economic grievances by themselves do not lead working classes to adopt revolutionary ideologies, as Lenin famously argued when attacking economism in *What Is to Be Done?* What matters is the degree of repressiveness of the state regime, the extent to which, to put the matter differently, states continue to draw upon an absolutist tradition. One key point deserves to be highlighted immediately. Variation inside the working class as a whole is by nation. To say this is to say that Marx's belief that the working class is a transnational class is false. There is here something of an asymmetry in class relations: workers are much more clearly caught inside their nations than are capitalists, whose mobility was noted in the last chapter.

This section has two purposes. First, we detail the ways in which state policy created different levels of political consciousness on the part of working classes. Second, we ask whether working classes so influenced their states that they may be held accountable for the wars of the twentieth century.

We can proceed best by placing four countries within a typology the polar points of which are inclusion and exclusion. At the liberal and inclusionary pole of typology stands the United States. Obviously there has been no socialism in the United States, in the sense of a Marxist-inspired mass party, drawing on substantial elements of the working class committed to fundamental social change. To understand this historical outcome it is necessary to come to terms with the distinctive manner in which class formation was fragmented and channelled in the post-Civil War era. The key feature of the American working-class experience during this period was the separation of the work-place from the politics of the larger community.[4] Struggles between workers and employers were played out in the factory, while local and national politics were organized around non-class coalitions and issues. This separation was crystallized in the United States of the nineteenth century by the emergence of trade unions and political machines. On the one hand, trade unions were largely detached from electoral politics. Union activities came to concentrate on the rather narrow concerns of the work-place. At the same time, urban political machines mobilized citizens on the basis of ethnic and neighborhood ties. Led by professional politicians, political machines built alliances that cut across social class, bringing together unionized and unskilled workers, middle-class groups in ethnic neighborhoods, and members of the business community.[5]

Three characteristics of the American situation explain why working-class organization developed in this way. First, the country was so diverse socially that it was, and is, very hard for any one cause to dominate it. This was true not just for the workers, but also for the political elite. The waves of immigration from Germany, Ireland and elsewhere ensured that cultural and ethnic diversity would typify the American work-place. Consequently, while working-class associations cut against this ethnic and cultural diversity, urban political machines built upon and reinforced it. To win elections, urban politicians had to gain the support of blocs of ethnic groups. Consequently, 'the opportunity for ethnic communities to enter the political process acted to solidify group

consciousness and to perpetuate the division of the city, demo-
graphically and politically, into ethnic components'.[6] Not only did
the ethnic pluralism constrain working-class organization, but the
partisan electoral institutions of the day found these divisions useful
blocs with which to build alliances. Second, class struggles took
place only in the industrial arena because the state was not
systematically opposed to the working class. The American revolution had been made by small farmers and artisans quite as much as
by landowners and merchants. In consequence, *white* adult males
quickly gained citizenship rights:

> By the early 1840s all of them, in all states, possessed the vote – fifty
> years earlier than anywhere else, fifty years before the emergence of
> a powerful labour movement. Thus the political demands of labour
> could be gradually expressed as an interest group *within* an existing
> political constitution and competitive party system.[7]

These citizenship rights were much extended as the result of the
mass participation in the armies of the Civil War.[8] The peculiarity of
the American situation is that a labour movement was never
involved in seeking citizenship rights; these were either enshrined in
the very idea of America, or achieved early on as the result of
conscription warfare. This is important since the salience of a
working class is likely to depend upon the extent to which it was
involved in the struggle for citizenship.[9] Finally, the decentraliz-
ation and fragmentation of the American state also affected
working-class formation. The nineteenth-century American political system of 'courts and party' was relatively underdeveloped in
comparative terms.[10] Just as the demand for a vote was not a central
feature of working-class struggle, the absence of a strong, centralized government removed the state as an object of attack.
Government became a vehicle for the mobilization of workers and
other citizens; it was a means of political incorporation. Citizenship
and electoral democracy came before, not after, the rise of a
bureaucratic state; there was no 'old regime' to overturn.

It is worth pausing for a moment to assess this liberal polar
position. Since the 1930s European historians and social scientists
have investigated the question of 'why is there no socialism in the
United States', to use the title of the striking book on the subject by
Werner Sombart[11]. Now this phrasing suggests that the United
States is peculiar, a deviation from the norm properly understood
by Marxism, in which an ever more organized working class girds up

its loins so as to join battle with capitalism, in order to achieve socialism. This way of putting the matter may be entirely wrong. If there is a 'natural' norm, perhaps it is that of the United States.[12] Louis Hartz put the matter neatly when arguing that it was only labour movements in societies with a feudal past that became revolutionary: no newly settled land – Argentina, the United States or Australia – developed a Marxist movement of any significance, fundamentally because their respective states remained liberal.[13]

The British case stands fairly close to this polar position. We have seen that the British state's history had made it generally liberal. It seemed for a short while, however, as if fear of the revolution in France would lead to generalized repression. Interestingly, this repressive drive did not last for long in Britain: the Combination Acts were repealed in 1824, while the franchise was first extended in 1832. The character of the British state explains this development:

> England's whole previous history, her reliance on a navy instead of an army, on unpaid justices of the peace instead of royal officials, had put in the hands of the central government a repressive apparatus much weaker than that possessed by the strong continental monarchies . . . The push towards industrialism had begun much earlier in England and was to render unnecessary for the English bourgeoisie any great dependence on the crown and the landed aristocracy. Finally, the landed upper classes themselves did not need to repress the peasants. Mainly they wanted to get them out of the way in order to go over to commercial farming; by and large, economic measures would be enough to provide the labour force they needed. Succeeding economically in this particular fashion, they had little need to resort to repressive political measures to continue their leadership.[14]

What Barrington Moore is stressing here is that capitalist society clearly pre-dated the emergence of industrial organization, and hence of the working class. The feudal past was not a dominant factor of the present, and capitalist society certainly did not have to be created under the active aegis of this legacy.

The presence of a liberal state in Britain, that is, a state not deliberately seeking to repress working-class organizations, made it rational for workers to concentrate their struggles, once repressive laws had been repealed, inside the work-place rather than against the state itself. Perhaps a certain softness to the British system had resulted from it being the first industrial nation; it was not necessary to push conflicts to any absolute extreme since there was enough money in the system to buy off discontent. Probably crucial, however, was a striking, virtuous and self-reinforcing cycle of expectations. Liberal politics bred industrial conflict rather than no-holds-barred political struggle. Yet it was perhaps the very absence of political struggle that encouraged the retention of liberal politics in the first place. This cycle can best be broken into by considering the franchise. As late as 1914, Britain was not a democratic society in the sense that suffrage had not been extended very far – certainly nothing like far enough to equal the near universal adult male suffrage of France, Germany and the United States. This was important. On the one hand, it limited the fears of the middle classes: they might have to face industrial militancy but they did not have to reckon with a politically motivated working-class capable of creating a new form of society – and that was precisely the fear that dogged many of their continental European counterparts. On the other hand, it created a sense of loyalty among the working class. Workers had to fight for citizenship rights, and the fact that these were not complete gave them a sense of identity.

These comments about the British case can be drawn together by considering Arthur Henderson and the Labour Party he did so much to shape. Ross McKibbin has noted that Henderson was (indirectly) a founder of Newcastle United Football Club, a distinguished Methodist lay preacher, and a prominent figure in lawn bowls – all in addition to his role as organizer of the Labour Party.[15] This neatly captures the strong and entirely autonomous associations of British labour; it was an estate of the realm with its own life – it was not that much bothered with politics. Accordingly, it fought loyally in the First World War, and there was not much sign that significant sections within it harboured notions of the nation of great distinctiveness. During the war, the trade unions became very embittered by those middle-class socialists who criticized a conflict in which their fellows were dying. Thus when the Labour Party finally gained a constitution in 1918, it was no accident that the unions ensured, through instituting the 'block vote' at party conferences, that they, rather than those middle-class socialists, would control the ultimate destiny of the party – as is still the case.[16] This was not a socialist party; it deserved its name – a *labour* party.

At this point, let us move towards the other end of the scale. Countries that clustered towards that end were those with an absolutist past and with traditional *anciens régimes* in place. The states of such societies wished, not least for reasons of military competition, to 'revolutionize their societies from above', that is, to modernize their economies while keeping their traditional social structures intact. The extent to which such a mixture was feasible is an issue which will concern us in Chapter 5.

The absolutely polar position was that of late nineteenth- and early twentieth-century Tsarist autocracy. It is certainly the case that the peasant seizure of land in 1917 was a vital factor making revolution possible, not least because it thereby made it impossible for reactionary forces to be recruited in the countryside so as to put down the social experiments in St Petersburg and Moscow. It is equally true that defeat in war debilitated the establishment. Nevertheless, there were genuinely revolutionary pressures for many years before this, and they originated from the working class of St Petersburg and Moscow. Interestingly, the workers involved were for once far more radical than their leaders, and at crucial moments even the Bolshevik Party was following rather than leading its workers. This is ironical given Lenin's analysis of economism in *What Is to Be Done?*, although it is always important to remember that Lenin's intellectual work was subsumed to his career as a revolutionary – by 1917 he no longer subscribed to his earlier pamphlet. Workers made a vital contribution to revolution: the Russian revolution probably deserves to be called the only working-class revolution in world history, although honourable mention in the dispatches of the left should be accorded to the German working-class's attempted revolution of 1919.

Tsarist autocratic government sought to be the father of all the people. A consequence of this was that it was suspicious, in a manner reminiscent of Imperial China, of every intermediary organization and grouping that stood between it and the people. This political culture provided very poor soil for capitalism. There was no tradition of private property, a limited legal tradition and none of the contractualistic tradition that had characterized feudal Europe. At the end of the nineteenth century, a furious debate took place between those who wished to Westernize Russia and those who wished to remain loyal to native traditions. Neither side definitively won this debate, and the Russian state consequently prevaricated between two options; in so doing it managed to get the worst of both worlds. The Westernizers introduced capitalism, but were unable, despite several government reports, to introduce the basic union organization that might have limited class conflict to the work-place.[17] On the occasions when this policy was tried, most notably immediately after the 1905 revolution, it seemed as if it was likely to prove successful.[18] However, the policy was not consistently maintained. The traditionalists tried to integrate the workers directly with the state, as in the Zubatov movement. One important consequence of the failure of this movement was that the workers, whose hopes had been raised by the state, blamed the state rather than the employers or the market. This was one factor that explains why the autocracy eventually moved towards a policy of total repression. Its own policy produced workers with revolutionary political consciousness. Such workers had little choice; they had to destroy the autocracy before anything else would be possible.

The bureaucratic authoritarianism of Imperial Germany was quite different from this. The German state never tried to undermine the hierarchical principle on which capitalism depended; it had none of that monarchic populism which so raised the expectations of Russian workers. This combination of authoritarianism with capitalism suited leading social classes. The grain-exporting, highly militaristic Junkers could assert their interests because of their overrepresentation in the estates system of Prussia. This power enabled them to demand agricultural protection, something which in turn helped sustain their position. The situation was the exact opposite of that of England: there the aristocracy had less entrenched power, and anyway, being already heavily involved in commerce, had much less to lose. The German bourgeoisie also differed from its British counterpart in being fundamentally loyal to an authoritarian state. Such loyalty is not hard to explain. Prussia had united Germany. This appealed to the middle classes both for nationalistic and economistic reasons; all business interests benefited from the creation, initially via the *Zollverein*, of national markets and a state-led drive towards industrialization, though heavy industrialists did particularly well from tariff protection. Equally importantly, the state provided the legal infrastructure on which capitalism depended, and was generally solicitous of its needs and interests.[19] This is not to say that the bourgeoisie did not even attempt to establish liberal political rule. But, such attempts as were made foundered on the basis of regional divisions which Bismarck used to devastating effect.[20] However, there is no doubt about the brute generalization that has to be made about such a late developmental strategy: it directly contradicts the liberal claim that capitalism and freedom go hand in hand. That beneficent combination characterized the first emergence of capitalism; the imitation of the same split capitalism and liberalism asunder.

In Imperial Germany a vicious cycle in the relations of state and society existed which contrasts neatly with the British situation. The Wilhelmine state tried to co-opt the working class with the carrot of the franchise and welfare legislation, and to scare it by means of various sticks, the most important of which were the anti-socialist laws that operated between 1878 and 1890. It was the latter that proved crucial in determining the character of the German working class. Workers were forced into political conflict with the state since the regulations of the latter prevented it from conducting its affairs on the purely industrial front. A consequence of the attraction of workers to socialism was that large elements of the middle class developed a bunker-type mentality; they felt so threatened that they embraced the authoritarian state with ever greater fervour. It is very important to realize that these fears were made the more realistic because of the presence of mass suffrage. The position as a whole is clear. Political repression was a dangerous route to follow. Experience of prison, rather than of low wages, gave bitterness to social action, while the presence of a repressive state necessitated that action taking a political form. By the end of the century an authoritarian state had bred the largest and best organized labour movement in Europe, although that movement was not revolutionary, preferring instead forceful and respectable reformism.

Whatever the differences in levels of political consciousness, one single generalization stands in regard to whether working classes' pressure occasions geopolitical conflict. The working class of every one of these states was prepared to go to war for its country in 1914. The British and American elite were not especially concerned with working-class pressure when thinking of foreign policy matters, and the same claim can be made in the Russian case. Some revisionist historians have argued, however, that German policy-makers were deeply influenced by the working-class. They have claimed that domestic fear of the working classes encouraged the elite to seek national unity by engaging in an aggressive external policy.[21] Some politicians did use language which suggested such fears, and there is accordingly an element of truth to this position. But the revisionists have themselves been revised! Detailed consideration of the evidence suggests that fears expressed were often 'put on' for domestic reasons, as in 1912, when a socialist scare proved highly effective in dealing with the most intransigent party of the time, that of the traditional right. In private, different sentiments were expressed: Chancellor Bethmann-Hollweg, for example, was certain that war would not avoid but actually *cause* social revolution.[22] Most importantly, however, the political elite felt that labour could be relied upon as far as foreign policy-making was concerned, and the test of war showed that this estimation was valid.

We will see later in this chapter that our general typology has to be amended if we are to understand the relations of workers to states in those societies which experienced revolutionary turbulence brought on by defeat in war. Nevertheless, this is a good moment at which to highlight the variables at work in it. The liberal end of the typology is one in which full political and social pluralism is permitted; the autocratic pole seeks to destroy both of these qualities. It is worth noting immediately an absolutely vital issue that follows from this typology. Michael Mann has very specifically argued that the combination of capital with authority was widely admired in 1914, and that there is every chance that it would have had continued success; this is to claim that the diversity of state–capitalist combinations was likely to continue.[23] This diversity was, however, destroyed in war. There is no doubt but that capitalists did ally themselves with authoritarian regimes, most notably in Germany; this undermines the link between commerce and liberty that had characterized the early modern experience in Europe. However, there are good reasons, examined in Chapter 5, for believing that late industrialism and geopolitical competition may move societies towards the recognition of civil society, and thereby towards softer political rule.

Traders and heroes

If the views and activities of the working class were not responsible for that increase in geopolitical tension that eventually led to the First World War, is it the case that the other major capitalist class played a major role in causing that? What truth is there to the contention of Lenin that that war had its origin in the nature of capitalism? In order to answer this question, a crucial distinction about the nature of capitalism must be reiterated.

Capitalist society was larger than any single state in 1914, as it has been before and is today. If the workings of that larger society depended upon international exchange, then it would seem on a priori grounds extremely unlikely that capitalists would favour war. This case was argued by Norman Angell in *The Great Illusion* in 1909. He insisted that war would bring economic disaster to those who won as much as to those who lost, and that 'the capitalist has no country, and he knows, if he be of the modern type, that arms and conquests and jugglery with frontiers serves no ends of his, and may very well defeat them'.[24] There is some evidence to back up this argument. Arms manufacturers gained most of their profits from sales outside their own nations, and their interest lay in an arms race rather than in actual war.[25] More importantly, international bankers were well aware of how much they benefited from free trade. This led the head of the London Rothschilds to try and persuade *The Times* not to encourage British support for France and Russia during the July crisis of 1914.[26] Furthermore, industrialists, too, stood to lose from war: ironically, in the decade before 1914, Britain became Germany's best customer and Germany the second best market for British goods.[27] These are examples of international capitalist logic being opposed to war. However, it is quite obvious that this logic was not very powerful. Capitalists might inhabit a larger society, but they had no real capacity to control the behaviour of states within it. This point can be put in a slightly different way. The majority of capitalists were, in this crucial matter, members of their particular nation states.

The fact that capitalists compete via nations is by no means inevitable; it is a reflection of the fact that capitalist society has no single state. But if we forget this problem, so fundamental for Marxism, it remains possible to assess whether capitalism caused war in 1914 in a different way: were European states driven by the needs of their capitalists into a foreign policy that resulted in war? This is a Marxist theory in two obvious senses. On the one hand, it is loyal to the tradition of Marxism which stresses that the problems of capitalism result from its anarchic character. On the other hand, it presumes that states serve the needs of their capitalists. It is very important, of course, to note that two rather different theories, only one of which is Marxist, lurk behind this simple statement. The first suggests that the state is controlled, in more or less complicated ways, by capitalists; this tradition does not allow any ultimate autonomy for state behaviour. The second theory sees the state as being in control – as an autonomous agent seeking to increase its own economic power by various geoeconomic strategies. Much of the following analysis revolves around this theoretically vital distinction.

Marxist work that has been done in this area develops from the view that imperialist acquisitions are necessary for national capitalists, and hence were the 'hidden agenda' of conflict that led to the First World War. This cannot be true in any simple şense. The scramble for Africa had been at its peak in the 1880s, and it had certainly not occasioned war between France and Britain; very much to the contrary, the imperial rivalries of these countries had been solved amicably. Furthermore, modern scholars have pointed out that formal imperialism was not simply the result of Western desires and ambitions; involvement was often forced upon rather reluctant Western powers by proto-nationalist movements.[28] There is another general consideration, and it has even greater importance. French colonies were not necessary to French capitalists either for new markets or as new places in which to invest. What is most striking about the majority of French capitalists at the turn of the century is that they were unwilling to invest in the colonies; certainly these colonies, given their poverty, presented few opportunities for trade. French capitalists preferred to invest in Russia, since development there was capable of realising large profits.[29] The conclusion to be drawn from this is banal but clear. French imperialism was not 'caused' by the objective needs of capitalists themselves. The German situation was similar. German economic success arose from trading in advanced markets. Certainly German capitalism was not about to perish for lack of the Belgian Congo, the prize most sought by German imperialistic statesmen! Even the British situation was not much different. Lower economic returns came from the colonies, including India, than from investments in, for example, Argentina; and in the long run, trading in an underdeveloped market proved disastrous for the British economy, allowing it to stagnate in technological terms.[30] The surest way in which Germany could have ensured the loss of British ascendancy was to have waited for it to exhaust itself by means of increased colonial expenditure. This would have happened quickly had Chamberlain's catastrophic plan for Imperial Preference been adopted; and it would have happened anyway as the result of an increase in nationalist demands. Certainly, there was nothing about the way in which the international political economy was working in 1914 to suggest anything other than that Germany's economy would continue to become ever more successful.

It would, however, be unsatisfactory to leave matters at this point. We have been speaking the logical language of neoclassical economics. Two considerations necessitate scepticism about the approach. First, sociologists have rightly made much of the fact that what is believed to be real is real in its consequences. By process of analogy, it can be argued that in economics what matters more than 'the facts' is what people *believe* to be the facts. In this connection, it is useful to make a distinction between two different senses in which one can speak of structure in social science. Some structures, notably demographic and economic ones, can only be discovered, so to speak, after the event by social scientists themselves; historical actors are blind to their reality. Hence it behoves the social scientist to spend more time dealing with structure in the rather different sense of working out what particular views were held by specific groups in order to establish a type of power-accounting explanation of why one rather than another triumphed. To make this distinction is to note a difference, in the matter of imperialism, between 'causes' and 'reasons': the former were not present, but the latter had great importance. Second, we need to remember the argument of Hobson and of Marxism, that a foreign economic policy that does not help a national economy as a whole may, nevertheless, be in the self-interest of a few capitalist actors. These points may, of course, be at odds with each other: the former questions the very nature of economic rationality while the latter depends on it.

At the end of the nineteenth century two geoeconomic strategies had come to the fore, as Werner Sombart emphasized in a book whose title stands at the head of this section.[31] The two strategies can initially be looked at in abstract terms. The first strategy, that of economic liberalism, sought interdependence between nations by allowing the principles of the market, including the benefits to be brought by comparative advantage, full rein. The intention of this strategy was to insist that politics be governed by what was happening in the economic structure of society. If this strategy sought to maximize wealth, its alternative sought to maximize security. Dependence on the market would mean that no single state would have full control over its destiny: access to markets might be cut off, while strategically important industries might not be available for purposes of mobilization. Britain had pioneered the trading strategy: it favoured open world markets, and accordingly allowed for open access to its imperial possessions. In the middle of the nineteenth century, it seemed as if this strategy was gaining ground everywhere. Germany had followed the Listian principle of protecting its nascent industries, but at this time it removed those tariffs.[32] However, realists rightly stress that the initial drive for industrialization has been often provided by the state, and that this is very largely for reasons of its own military security. This contributed to the disruption of liberal hopes that the hidden hand of economic growth would bring political harmony. The military arguments for industrialization led itself to an increase in world surplus capacity, something which encouraged trade rivalry.[33] This was much exacerbated by economic depression in the 1870s. At that time, Germany produced a complete protectionist and mercantilist vision seeking to maximize security. This strategy insisted on the retention of militarily important food production and industries, even when this was 'economically irrational'.

Now that these two strategies have been distinguished, it becomes important to inquire about their inner workings. In the British case there was straightforward unity between capitalism and the foreign policy elite; the latter depended on the former for the brutally obvious reason that British state power resulted from its trading position. The German case was more complex. Was German policy adopted because of the pressure of capitalists, or was it autonomously chosen by the state? No simple answer can be given to this question. Certainly the unholy alliance of Junkers and heavy industrialists, both of whom demanded protection in the late 1870s, was of exceptional importance in influencing the state. It was, of course, less capitalism *per se* than particular capitalists, in the sense that Hobson and many later Marxists made familiar, who benefited from protection and, after 1897, from naval construction. Moreover, the Junkers had their views massively magnified by the structure of the political system in Germany, as was clearly seen when they undermined Caprivi's attempt to move the German state closer towards a British trading strategy. None the less, quite as important was the militarist strategy of the German state. Foreign policy leaders wished to preserve key industries for reasons of geopolitical security. In addition, however, it must be remembered that the decision to build a navy was popular with reformist domestic groups, including the Social Democrats, for an entirely different reason: they supported this policy and opposed the alternative plan for an expansion of the army because they feared the latter could be used for domestic repression.

An analytic point of great importance, first noticed by Schumpeter, needs to be highlighted at this point. Capitalists like to be left alone so as to make money; they do not normally produce their own geopolitical vision. If *some* capitalists helped to create the German geoeconomic strategy of *Weltpolitik* because it was in their interest to do so, it is very important indeed to remember that many German capitalists who had nothing to gain economically from empire supported this policy quite as much. Capitalists sometimes accede to the visions propagated by intellectuals and politicians; they do not always calculate their interests in narrowly monetary terms, being as prone to political romanticism as other social actors. The point can be formulated in a different way: German capitalists were Germans before they were businessmen. States can, in other words, interfere with the pure logic of larger capitalist society. Imperialism is the classic instance of such interference, but the geoeconomic plans created by German state leaders are another. Perhaps acceptance of the latter is scarcely surprising: German sovereignty and self-determination had nearly been destroyed by Napoleon, and geoeconomic plans had only taken on a coherent – and, for capitalists, highly advantageous – form under Bismarck.

It should be noted in addition that the German state had a good deal of autonomy, not least because it could always balance between different social groups, regions or classes. Bismarck after 1870 and von Bülow throughout his chancellorship were, *and were able to be*, both cautious and pragmatic. Bethmann-Hollweg could have behaved with equal caution, and certainly there were no explicit instructions from capitalists telling him what to do; he was not a puppet controlled by economic interests. What is noticeable is how inept the political elite was at calculating its own interests. Most obviously, Britain had not shown any serious sign of closing off her markets, and it would anyway have been possible to make bilateral agreements, as the United States did in 1912, to open the German market more completely to Britain and thereby to ensure free trade in general had British pressure made this necessary.[34] Furthermore, if we accept, as we must, that the German geoeconomic strategy came to be based on the belief that it was necessary to acquire markets for the longer run, the manner in which this strategy was put into effect was remarkably clumsy. Some of the blame for this must be laid at Bismarck's door: his boasts of machiavellianism and of admiration for a neo-Nietzschean struggle for survival created general distrust. But it was Bethmann-Hollweg who eventually made the fundamental mistake of going to war against three, and eventually four, major powers, and in a war on two fronts. The lack of calculation certainly reflected the absence of a unified structure of command in the German state. That Germany found itself in the same position by 1941 is, of course, as extraordinary as it was decisive for the shape of twentieth-century history.

This is a good moment to draw together evidence to assess the liberal claim that a liberal political regime in Germany would have been peaceful. It is true that liberal states did not fight against each other during the two world wars, although the presence of Russia on the side of the allies in both conflicts reminds us that the wars themselves were as much concerned with geopolitical issues as with the fate of liberalism. Nevertheless, there is some truth to the detailed argumentation underlying this contention. The voice of heavy industry and of the Junkers was much enhanced by the peculiarities of the German political system. But the strength of that voice does not finally account for German policy, and there are other good reasons for showing a certain wariness to the liberal claim. The sharing of a liberal system had not prevented Britain and France from contemplating war over colonial possessions, just as the sharing of many cultural patterns and economic interests (the latter being, admittedly, unable to express themselves fully because of the German political system) did not prevent war between Germany and Britain. One suspects that the peaceful change that took place in the relations of Britain and the United States had less to do with shared economic or political interests than geography: Germany was just too close for Britain to be accommodated in the same manner. Finally, we must note that liberalism had further costs to it. Eyre Crowe's famous memorandum to Sir Edward Grey, then the Liberal Foreign Secretary, had correctly identified German *Weltpolitik*, and had suggested that it might be controlled by a clear guarantee by Britain of French territorial integrity. Such a guarantee could not be given by the party of Cobden, traditionally suspicious of foreign entanglements; a Conservative administration might have managed Britain's geopolitical situation rather better.

The causes of the war should not all be placed in Germany's camp, even though the consensus of current scholarship places most blame on Germany. Adjustment in the balance of power to take account of the uneven development of capitalism is a two-way process, and Britain was not good at dealing with the crisis of transition, even though protectionism and imperial free trade *were* resisted. Perhaps no fundamental rapprochement was possible. Britain's rise to power had been based on overseas trade. It was always likely that other powers would seek to emulate Britain, and to demand a place in the sun. This caused Britain terrible problems.

It made it necessary, above all, to move from the optional strategy of having a non-territorial empire of free trade to the acquisition and maintenance of an increasingly expensive formal empire.[35] Britain was slow at offering to give some of its colonies away to its principal rival, but the essential damage had really been done much earlier when Britain turned European politics into world politics. Once Britain was genuinely dependent on international trade, not least for its own food, it was always likely to resist a naval challenge. None the less, British complaints about German economic success were sometimes unwise; German goods were successful because they were better, and this had little to do with tariffs – as some British commentators, to their credit, realized. More effort should have been made to understand the desire to protect domestic grain: if a state wishes to pay more for its supplies, there is much to be said in favour of allowing it to do so, although it does require economic adjustment on the part of the country with cheap surplus. Finally, it is worth remembering that the forces of nationalism in Britain were almost as substantial as they were in Germany: the Fleet was admired throughout society, and the war was initially widely welcomed.

Bolsheviks, Fascists and the totalitarian state

A great deal of space has been devoted to looking at the origins of the First World War, for the simplest of reasons: the two world wars took place in chain reaction, that is, the seeds of the Second World War were sown in the outcome of the First. What mattered most was that defeat in war encouraged revolutionary turbulence. Let us look in turn at the two great revolutionary systems of the inter-war years.

Defeat of Tsarist Russia led to a transfer of loyalty from nation to class. This opening made possible the victory of the Bolsheviks. As is well known, Lenin had been extremely impressed by the mobilized and centralized war economy of Imperial Germany, but he did not manage to introduce this system during his lifetime. Instead the initial period of 'War Communism' was succeeded by a less coercive, more market-orientated 'New Economic Policy'. There has been much argument as to whether this latter model could have been successful, and thus have allowed for a more liberal socialist strategy of modernization.[36] While it is true that such a policy might have worked in the long run, it is noticeable that the revolutionaries, who had been attacked by the West in the years after 1918, came increasingly to feel that they might not have a longer run: the destruction of the Chinese Communists in 1927 encouraged the first of Stalin's drives into the countryside. As Bukharin had predicted, state coercion proved catastrophic in many ways: the size of the harvest fell dramatically and millions of animals were slaughtered. But this did not matter for the state, which massively increased its share of the harvest. It was this piece of brutal coercion that allowed the full Soviet model of industrialization to be put into place. The contours of the model are familiar: complete central planning, the relative suppression of classes and dominance by a single party, armed with a Promethean ideology used to transform a national society which has withdrawn from the world market. Adoption of this model in the Soviet Union allowed for a forcible solution to the peasant problem, and for massive investment in heavy industry. Consumer preferences would have been to do without this investment: it was made possible by the fact that the Soviet model was based on dictatorship.

Germany came close to a leftist revolution in 1919, but the established forces remained in sufficient array to put this down. It is important to note that it was a Social Democratic government which was responsible for putting down a communist rebellion; this made it impossible thereafter for a united left to stand together in Germany to protect Weimar democracy. This was the first of a series of conjunctural factors that eventually led to revolution from the right. If Hitler found much support among ex-servicemen and the members of the 'service class' which was particularly opposed to communism – then, it should be recalled, a genuine force for international revolution – it is important to remember that he gained his access to power as the result of the behaviour of established social forces. This is not to say that fascism was, as Marxism has it, merely the 'agency' for capitalism. Fascism did not take root in the leading capitalist societies of the United States and Britain, but it did take a significant hold in Romania, despite that country being essentially agrarian! Fascism is best seen as a pathology of forced modernization: memories of pre-industrial 'harmony', of '*Kinder, Küche, Kirche*', were revived in an industrial country to create the anti-liberal ideology of reactionary modernism.[37] But if only von Thyssen actively helped the Nazis from early on, his business colleagues preferring to support the parties of the right, it is extremely noticeable that the capitalist middle classes were no friends to Weimar: they gave it no positive support and showed extreme resentment to a regime that initially raised the wages of the working class. However, what ultimately mattered more than this lack of support was the active involvement of sections of the traditional elite, most notably von Papen, in putting Hitler into power.

In the inter-war years, the notion of totalitarianism was created on the grounds that both these revolutionary systems shared fundamental features.[38] With hindsight, it can be seen that this label should be applied with care. There were fundamental differences between Nazism and Stalinism: the bases of social support for the two systems were entirely different, while the latter at least paid attention to universal moral norms – which did not prevent it killing even more of its own citizens. Equally importantly, the concept is misused if it is deemed to apply to the Soviet Union *per se*, rather than to the years between 1928 and 1953. But if these limitations are accepted, the concept can be accepted as veridical. Both states hated nothing so much as liberalism; each sought to organize both economy and society on the basis of an all-embracing ideology, one-party rule, and terror. These systems make the polar scale of worker–state relations used earlier in this chapter redundant. In that scale, the authoritarian end sought simply to exclude the working class from political participation. Franco and Mussolini more or less continued that tack. But both Nazism and Bolshevism sought to mobilize the masses rather than to keep them quiet. Of course, much of the support that was given to these regimes depended upon their instrumental achievements; these were the only states in the inter-war years which found an answer to the problem of unemployment.

The nature of regimes absolutely justifies the single most important point made about the state by the liberal tradition. Uncontrolled political power can and did lead to catastrophe, both inside these societies and for the world. Pace Marxism, the nature of regimes matters. Marxists effectively admit this in allowing that 'a cult of personality' – surely a notion absolutely divorced from any version of historical *materialism* – distorted Soviet history. If there is comfort for liberalism in this judgement, the events of the inter-war years in other respects cast considerable doubt upon aspects of its conception of the relations between state and society. Most obviously, the connection posited, more or less closely, by liberals between capitalism and liberalism seemed to make less and less sense in these years. Capitalists showed passive resistance to Weimar. But another point deserves equal emphasis. If liberals can occasionally be too harsh to states with different political regimes, they can also fail to be harsh enough. There is much to criticize about this sort of liberal behaviour in the inter-war years, as E. H. Carr so forcefully suggested in 1939.[39] Woodrow Wilson's version of Gladstonian morality was felt at Versailles in the demand that Germany accept moral guilt for having started a war. This was surely a highly questionable policy to adopt. Germans did not feel guilt for having indulged in what had been the traditional recourse of European states over centuries; they thereby gained a justified sense of resentment upon which Hitler was later successfully to feed. This is not to say that all liberals were behind the Versailles Treaty; on the contrary, most liberals condemned the harsh terms imposed on Germany, and felt that real liberal principles had been flouted. The classic statement of this view was Keynes's *The Economic Consequences of the Peace* which argued, brilliantly and passionately, that the treaty was not only vindictive but also self-defeating: how could the Allies both ruin the German economy – thereby hurting their own export industries! – and demand the payment of reparations?[40] There was indeed much to be said for a liberal peace, and this part of Keynes's argument retains force. However, we live in an imperfect world, and have to act in situations which are sullied and impure. In 1919 the fears of the French ruled out of court a generous peace. By and large, liberals failed to realize this. Throughout the inter-war years, everything that was best in their mentality told them that Germany had just claims to make; the liberal conscience, in other words, created a climate in which appeasement flourished.[41] Given that a generous peace treaty was impossible in 1919, there was much to be said for the creation of a genuinely Carthaginian peace, that is, a peace which would not allow Germany to start another war. As it was, the worst possible result was achieved: the creation of a peace treaty which was neither respected nor enforced. The liberal conscience thus played some part in making the Second World War possible. Norman Angell, one of the exemplars of liberal morality, realized this late in life when he admitted that although 'Balance of Power had a bad smell with nearly all Liberals, including this one . . . later on [they] came to see that power politics [was] the politics of not being overpowered'.[42] If it is very much to the credit of liberalism that some sort of Kantian solidarity between liberal states does seem to have been present in the historical record, this has to be weighed against the lack of realism – understood both as sense and as the branch of political science that has appropriated this title – with which it has often conducted its affairs with non-liberal states.

Conclusion

Our analysis has depended most upon the insights of the realist tradition, but we have added to this the difficult tasks statesmen faced because of uneven growth within capitalism. At the same time, it has been necessary to add to realism considerations from Marxism and liberalism. One element in the coalition that created German state policy at the end of the nineteenth century was, as Marxists stress, clearly that of major capitalists, concerned to protect their own interests; we cannot, in other words, completely understand German policy without raising the impact of this societal force. Liberalism does not gain such clear support from the evidence we have examined. The human costs of totalitarian regimes, of course, lend salience to liberalism's philosophy of history. More particularly, the normative hopes of liberalism gain limited support from the counter-factual proposition that a more liberal German political system might have been more peaceful; it is certainly important in this connection to note that the autonomy of the state would have been increased by a more representative political system. However, domestic popular pressure in Britain played some part in limiting the autonomous room for manoeuvre of Sir Edward Grey. Liberal regimes seem to have opportunities and costs attached to them.

These considerations lead almost inevitably to the subject matter of the next chapter. Has anything changed in the combination of capitalism and states to suggest that a repetition of disaster may be avoided? Are there novel features of the contemporary world polity that will allow the peoples of the contemporary world to escape the débâcle that engulfed previous generations of Europeans?

The Long Peace?

In this chapter we discuss the foundations and prospects of the peaceful settlement which has characterized relations between the major powers since 1945. One undoubted element in this situation is that of the bipolar conflict between the United States and the Soviet Union, and this is accorded due weight here. But every year that goes by makes it clearer that the geopolitical challenge of socialist society has been exaggerated, not least because very *few* countries have turned socialist; it is this which accounts for renewed interest in the relations between states *within* capitalist society. We begin by discussing the geopolitical and economic architecture of the American system, and describe the political coalition that stood behind it. We go on to consider the limited opportunities of many underveloped countries within this system, although we recognize the rapid advance of some of them, namely the Newly Industrializing Countries (NICs). We also analyse the flexible trading strategies of some advanced industrial nations. Can change and growth in capitalist society now be accommodated within a competitive system of states? This necessitates discussing the prospects of the United States within the international system which its geopolitical victory helped it to create. Is American economic leadership proving to be self-liquidating, as hegemonic stability theorists, bearing in mind the example of Britain, predict?

The American system

The United States was in an extraordinarily powerful position after the Second World War, and this enabled it to promote its own liberal conception of international order. These efforts led to a successful incorporation of West Germany and Japan into an

American-led system. But if capitalist society was unified under the auspices of an American grand strategy, it was with a host of compromises along the way: the American system was by no means pure. At the heart of American post-war economic designs were commercial and financial relations based on liberal multilateralism: governments were to abide by the discipline of the market and to facilitate domestic adjustment to international economic change. European officials, particularly the British, were weary of unadulterated liberal multilateralism, and in the economic diplomacy that followed the war, negotiations returned time and time again to one basic question: what was to be the scope of national autonomy in matters of economic policy? In settling this question, the United States and other capitalist nations were searching for ways to reconcile global liberalism and the emerging welfare state. We examine this process of reconciliation in planning policy, and then consider the balance of political forces in the post-war American state that allowed the rise of globalism.

The plans of Keynes and Dexter White for the post-war economic order discussed at Bretton Woods in 1944 both recognized the need to respect certain basic economic laws, most notably the need to have balanced international accounts. They differed over provision of liquidity and the allocation of responsibility for adjustment between creditor and debtor countries. The British emphasized the primacy of national control over fiscal and monetary policy, the importance of biasing the arrangements towards economic expansion, and the need for a large international reserve and relatively easy terms of access to adjustment funds.[1] In the settlement that followed, the more miserly American plan was pushed through. None the less, differences in interpretation persisted. American officials gave the impression to their public that the foundations of liberal multilateralism had been laid. Further funds would not be necessary for British economic reconstruction and a British commitment to non-discrimination had been achieved. British officials took home a different message: the transition period would be lengthy, employment and economic stability would be protected, and the American government would make the sacrifices necessary to ensure post-war economic expansion.[2]

In the negotiations and compromises that followed the Bretton Woods agreements, the United States came to accept a looser, less disciplined liberal multilateral system – a system that was congruent with domestic Keynesianism and the welfare state. For the most part this took the form of exemptions and abridgements in trade and financial arrangements. These compromises allowed for a larger measure of national economic autonomy and a stronger role for the state in pursuing full employment and social welfare; they resulted in what John Ruggie has termed 'embedded liberalism'. 'The task of postwar institutional reconstruction', Ruggie reasons, was to 'devise a framework which would safeguard and even aid the quest for domestic stability without, at the same time, triggering the mutually destructive external consequences that had plagued the interwar period'.[3] In other words, rules would be devised to allow for non-discrimination in commercial and monetary relations, but also to facilitate the consolidation of the welfare state. Ruggie argues that a loose consensus existed among the advanced states of capitalist society, even during the war, on the need to make compromises between liberal multilateralism and domestic inter-ventionism. This was true, however, only at the most general level. Embedded liberalism came into being quite gradually and in piecemeal fashion over the entire decade of the 1940s. European countries gave ground on the American insistence that multilateral-ism stand at the core of international economic arrangements. The United States came to accept the need to protect newly emerging Keynesian economic policies and the provisions of the welfare state. But these compromises were less in the nature of explicit agreements than they were a product of the failure of such instruments of liberal multilateralism as the Anglo-American Financial Agreement and the International Trade Organization.[4]

These plans depended upon allied states accepting certain key structural changes, and these too resulted from a combination of external pressure and internal agreement. The United States obviously used massive coercive power in reconstructing West Germany and Japan. However, it is insufficiently appreciated that the United States was as interventionist in other states which seemed in danger of slipping out of its orbit.[5] The fundamental policy of the United States was to establish a historic class compromise which ruled out the extreme right and the extreme left.[6] To that end it was prepared to finance centrist parties which sought such a settlement for their own reasons, and to use covert actions when that proved necessary. However, this settlement was not achieved at a stroke. It needed perceptions of an increasing geopolitical threat of the Soviet Union in 1946 and 1947 to make the United States come up with key funds in the Marshall Plan and a firm guarantee of military protection in the formation of NATO. This is another point at which it would be misleading to speak naively of the American system: the United States had not wanted to have a continental commitment to Europe, and it had wanted, as noted, a Europe open to its preferred multilateral norms; it ended up with NATO, and eventually with the European Economic Community.

A very particular coalition of domestic political groups stood behind American policy. It is scarcely surprising to discover that the American state was permeable to capitalist pressure; the liberalism of its foundation encouraged this, and it had had no long history of geopolitical involvement to create significant state capacity. Hence the earliest proponents of an American-led international order were businessmen and government officials who articulated from 1941, through the Council on Foreign Relations, a vision of a liberal multilateral economic order.[7] There was a genuine confluence of views between these groups, and it would be a mistake to try to draw an absolute analytic distinction between them. Many genuinely believed that free trade and peace went together; it was possible to serve others whilst serving oneself. None the less, we can distinguish to some extent between the behaviour of these different types of actor. The importance of the permeability of the state to capitalists distinctively in possession on *this* occasion of a sophisticated geopolitical sense, was particularly seen in the inclusion of certain areas of the Third World, most notably South-East Asia, as part of 'the national interest'; this probably reflected special interests more than an objective and neutral reckoning of American strategic needs. But this should not be taken to mean that state actors had no autonomy whatsoever. Several key foreign policy actors, most notably Roosevelt, Harriman and Acheson, had attended private school at Groton. They were made conscious there of the decline of Britain, and taught that their role would be to take over the leadership of the world – a role they felt all the more inclined to accept given the huge power of the United States at the end of the war. There was, in other words, a genuine foreign policy elite with goals of its own; its autonomy was seen in the fact that acceptance of European economic policies going against multi-lateralism was for traditional balance of power reasons. This elite had come to believe that world leadership was not just an option but a vital necessity; they considered that the failure of the United States to participate in world politics had exacerbated the crises of the inter-war years, and they thereby insisted that involvement might well be cheaper than isolation. But herein lay a great problem for internationalists of all sorts. The American people – and, in particular, voters with ethnic ancestries in Germany and Ireland – had long been suspicious of international involvements, and they had proved capable of delaying American entry into the Second World War. So if internationalist feeling on the part of key capitalists and key state actors was vital to the American system, so too was the creation of domestic support. The Truman administration managed to obtain this in a dramatic but highly particularistic manner. The Republican Congress elected in 1946 was at once anti-communist and keen to balance the budget. It proved possible to turn highly anti-communist Republicans such as Vandenberg, who himself faced re-election from mid-Western Polish-American voters, in an internationalist direction, and to split them from that fiscally cautious mainstream headed by Taft which was generally suspicious of foreign entanglements.[8] America's rise to globalism was very much a hit and miss affair.

The United States in effect created a grand strategy in the years after 1941. The fact that parts of the strategy were in place so early partly accounts for the unfolding dynamic of interaction with the Soviet Union that resulted in the cold war. The Soviet Union recognized the ambitions of the United States and accordingly increased in its own security demands and policies; this in turn made many American leaders interpret Soviet behaviour as more dangerous than was probably the case.[9] In this, the United States was dominated by what it felt to be historical lessons – above all, that appeasement would never work (an analogy whose exact appropriateness to changed circumstances was and is rather questionable). This was one origin of the extensiveness of the commitments of the United States within the system it did so much to create. A second source lay in the condition and behaviour of the Europeans. The collapse of Britain at this time left a genuine power vacuum, and Europeans preferred to fill it by asking the United States to provide defence for them rather than to act on their own: this was an empire by invitation.[10] Moreover, Europeans were edgy and nervous: the American involvement in South Korea was partly occasioned by the need to reassure Europeans of the commitment to NATO. But there was a third factor which explains not only the extensiveness of the American commitment, but also the inflexibility with which it came to be held. Foreign policy-makers gained domestic consent for internationalism by stressing a uniform communist threat – even though they did not themselves usually define world politics quite so crudely behind closed doors. George Kennan, in particular, soon came to recommend a flexible foreign policy that recognized that communism would become ever more split by nation, a factor which would allow for traditional balance of power politics rather than straightforward bipolar confrontation.[11] Domestic factors made it very hard to adopt such a flexible approach. Key officials such as Marshall and Acheson came under attack from McCarthyism for the loss of China, and this ensured thereafter that the political elite would be very chary about opening itself to the charge of having lost any piece of territory. This belief may have been false, but it was real, and it had consequences. Some of these concern the Third World, to which we now turn.

The politics of development

In the 1940s, the United States was a champion of self-determination and sovereignty for the less developed regions of the world. American pressure helped to ensure that one of the most noticeable changes made in the modern world polity has been the creation of new states. But while sovereign statehood has spread to what were once called the 'backward territories', economic advance has proved to be more difficult to achieve. In analysing the success and prospects of the American system, we begin by analysing the prospects for development among the least advantaged nations within that system. Let us begin by looking at the relationship between political regime and economic development in the abstract.

Adam Smith was right to note that the emergence of capitalism and liberal rule were connected. However, the natural and organic emergence of industrial society was unique; all industrialization thereafter has been, by definition, imitative. The directive – no lesser word will do – of modern history is that of speeding up industrialization. In these circumstances, the equation of commerce *and* liberty no longer holds, as we have already seen both in the bureaucratic authoritarianism of Imperial Germany and the state socialism pioneered by the Soviet Union. The generalization to be made about this whole situation is that *forced development entails dictatorship*.[12] A brief examination of the social engineering involved in rapid modernization will explain this harsh formula. Let

us consider two of the 'functional prerequisites' of the modern
industrial era.

The first of these is sectoral change. Most agrarian societies
require approximately 90 per cent of the work-force to act as
agricultural producers in order that a very small elite may be
supported. In contrast, most advanced societies now have primary
sectors under 10 per cent of their work-force, with several advanced
capitalist societies having less than 5 per cent so engaged. Although
it was never the case that a majority of the work-force in industrial
societies was engaged in the secondary industrial sector, this is not
to downplay the fundamental insight of Barrington Moore's *Social
Origins of Dictatorship and Democracy* that modernization, under
whatever political aegis, involves at least disciplining the peasantry
and at most forcibly removing it from the land.[13]

The second 'functional prerequisite' is nation-building. The
difficulties involved in nation-building can best be appreciated by
considering the situation of states that are entirely new. The citizens
of industrial society must have the capacity to communicate with
each other at an abstract level, preferably in a single language. This
necessitates all states, including those of the old heartland of
North-West Europe, creating schooling systems which both mobilize the people and give them the skills to participate in a literate and
technical society. It is important at this point, however, to make
certain distinctions. There is a world of difference between adding
some elements to an established nation state and creating such a
state in the first place. Less obvious but equally vital is the
distinction between types of country in the Third World. Imperial
Germany, Imperial Japan and Tsarist Russia were the first underdeveloped countries, but they had pre-existent patterns of literacy,
bureaucracy and authority on which to draw when reaching for the
modern world; the same is not true for the highly artificial states,
bounded, most notably in Africa, by those suspiciously straight
lines drawn up by nineteenth-century imperialists, which have no
traditions on which to draw and which have to deal, in contrast, with
a mass of differentiated tribes rather than a people with some sort of
culture based on a shared history.[14] Clearly the tasks of state- and
nation-building in these geopolitical artifices are absolutely massive. This distinction between types of country seeking to develop is
crucial and deserves further illustration. A consideration of their
rather different nationalisms can provide this. All nationalism is
reactive to the uneven diffusion of capitalism around the globe.

However, the nationalism of a Japan or a Germany amounts to being a true demand for self-determination in the sense that the myths of the nation have some historic validity; it is this which makes such nationalism genuinely popular. In contrast, the myths of previous national existence in a country such as Nigeria are without any substance whatever, and their appeal is accordingly limited. Such myths are propagated by native intellectuals, the blocking of whose vertical mobility by imperial rulers seems to be the principal mechanism occasioning such nationalism in the first place. In such cases, nationalism *is* nation-building, the creation of an entirely new shared identity for very disparate human material.

With an appreciation of these background conditions to socio-economic development, we can better comprehend the relationship between dictatorship and development by utilizing the distinction between infrastructural and despotic powers of the state. Nothing has been said here to show any positive liking of despotism. How marvellous it would be if India could move, as Europe did in the past, from a situation low in both despotism and infrastructure to one in which a democratic state ruled over an economically and socially advanced society! The extent to which this might be so remains a hotly debated topic.[15] But it is because this is unlikely to happen that despotism must be negatively endorsed *in so far as it helps to establish decent infrastructural conditions*, that is, the mobilization of the people in order that they may become part of a developed country. Such infrastructural capacity has clearly been enhanced by the despotic power of the Soviet, Chinese and Korean states. But it would be a great mistake to assert, and we are not so doing, that despotism *by itself* ensures development. Examples in both socialist and capitalist arenas – the Cambodia of Pol Pot and the Haiti of the Duvaliers – demonstrate that despotic powers may not be used to establish a modern society.

To argue that development requires the strengthening of the state goes against all liberal preconceptions. One reason why this argument should not really surprise us, however, is that the rise of the West was not, as we have seen, by any means stateless. Surely it is hypocritical of citizens in the contemporary West to expect the Third World to manage without strong states – albeit, as stressed, that strength needs to be of the right type – when they did not do so themselves? The normative policy implication of this point is straightfoward: the advanced societies should encourage state- and nation-building in the Third World.

The observation that strong states can facilitate development also challenges another perspective on socioeconomic change in the Third World, that of dependency theory.[16] Very few states have been able, largely because they lack resources and a large internal market, to withdraw from the world market; the increasing dynamism of that market makes it, moreover, more and more attractive to all countries that have left the world market – certainly to China, and probably to the Soviet Union as well, both of whom are well aware that isolation carries with it the price tag of slow economic growth. At the same time, the remarkable economic growth experienced by the NICs, particularly those in Asia, suggests that developing countries can find niches in the world economy within which successful strategies of development can be sustained. Yet we are again confronted with the important role that states can play in promoting policies of economic growth. Recent studies of economic development (or 'dependent development') give new weight to domestic political forces and policy choices of the state in explaining outcomes.[17] The lesson here is one observed by Stephan Haggard: 'Dependency is too frequently portrayed as a determinant international structure rather than as a set of shifting constraints within which states seek to maneuver.'[18]

It would be gravely mistaken, however, to leave matters at this point. For if some countries have developed, in sheer numerical terms most have not – and do not look likely to. International trade figures suggest, for example, that the world economy would scarcely notice if Africa disappeared off the face of the globe, a realization that has led some to begin to talk of a Fourth World. There are two broad sets of reasons which explain why some have been successful but most have failed. Allusion has already been made to the internal factors at work. Some states are made weak by the fact that they are entirely new, and stand at the head of societies composed of highly disparate peoples. The Japanese state was obviously in an entirely different position, and it had further advantages. The ability of capitalists to exit from national societies in the developing world may be disastrous, as is evident in the appalling fact that Latin America has been a net exporter of capital, as well as of skilled manpower, for many years. The Japanese elite did not have a reference group abroad, and had, moreover, linguistic difficulties; the result was that strategies of voice were preferred in Japan to those of exit.[19] The NICs vary quite radically in their domestic political and economic endowments and in the development strategies they pursue. But in each case the state has played a crucial role in economic transformation and export promotion. Among the Asian NICs, protectionist policies were used to protect infant industries, state-owned enterprises have selectively been used to promote industrial development, and an array of laws has been elaborated to influence the trade behaviour of multinational corporations. In ways that are still not fully understood, the states in these Asian NICs have pursued systematic economic management, selective import liberalization, and exchange rate and tax reform. Standing behind these instruments and policy packages, one finds a historical tradition that provided these countries with respect for bureaucratic intervention together, in some cases, with fundamental land reform, as pushed through by Japan in the years in which it had a territorial empire.

It is very depressing to realize that few countries in the Third World have anything like this sort of political and societal portfolio. There are external factors which make it uniquely hard for most Third World states to drag their societies into the modern world. We should not forget, to begin with, that the Third World has *not* seen much peace since 1945; rather, the fact that is has some room for manoeuvre between the superpowers and that it is without nuclear weapons systems of its own, has made it the heartland of classical wars of horrible intensity. This has affected development chances. The cost of modern weapons is now so great that it seriously impairs state attempts at mobilization: in 1984, Angola was forced to spend $133 per person on defence and a mere $49 per person on education.[20] Equally important, it has been the non-oil-producing developing countries which have been most severely hit by the rise in world oil prices: this has created indebtedness in Latin America and stymied growth everywhere – largely because basic development requires a massive growth in oil use.[21] More important still, dependency theory *is* correct to point to difficulties of industrialization within an already industrialized world. The fundamental fact is that industrialization now requires high levels of skill and capital equipment: the introduction of ever higher technology will unquestioningly place most of the developing world at an even greater disadvantage. Where European industrialization took place slowly on the basis of pre-existent craft industries, the speed of technological change means that this leisurely route is ruled out for contemporary developing states. Moreover, massive investment in basic industries which are then protected behind tariff walls, either in imitation of the 'Soviet model' or as 'import substituting industrialization', is becoming less and less successful. Unless a state can move with remarkable speed from protection towards opening to the world market, its internal resources will soon be spent supporting industrial plant which has become outdated and correspondingly expensive. It is highly noticeable in this regard that the Asian NICs force their industries to compete internationally, and encourage society as a whole, not least by the use of a myriad of independent economic bureaux, to take international market forces with the utmost seriousness.[22] One suspects that such flexibility is only possible for societies in which strong social infrastructures have already been established.[23] It may be possible for post-revolutionary China to adopt this strategy; it would, in contrast, prove disastrous for most African states.

One final topic must be addressed in this discussion of the politics of development. What is the likely political evolution of those societies which have made the transition to industrialism? Is there any chance, once the forced transition has been made, even in the absence of democracy, that a measure of 'softness' may come to characterize social and political relations? In order to answer this question, we need to examine the two principal versions of forced development seen in the modern world, that is, state socialism and authoritarian capitalism.

The geopolitical success of the Soviet Union in the Second World War led to its model of development being adopted in widely differing circumstances. Sometimes this was wholly inappropriate, as in China, where the attempt to change the sectoral shape of a society with a huge population led to massive famines as early as 1958. We know far too little about diversity within socialist society, but we cannot help but note that it has not remained static. What is at issue here is more than the reaction, proclaimed by Khrushchev, against the Stalinist 'cult of personality'. Structural problems have dogged the Soviet model over time, three of which can usefully be identified. First and most embarrassing, the openness of which socialist society once boasted is being eroded. Peasant social mobility was caused by destruction of traditional elites and, crucially, by the fact that industrialization increased the number of white-collar jobs by changing the occupational structure. Second, central planning is much more efficacious at boosting early industrialization than it is at managing a complex late industrial economy, as is evident in the slowing of socialist growth rates and in the fact that the exports of the Soviet Union largely consist, as do those of many Third World countries, of non-manufactured goods. The costs of trying to suppress, rather than to co-operate with, independent civil society groups are now apparent to all. Finally, it is apparent that the parties of all advanced state socialist societies face problems of legitimation. All Bolshevik parties are now schizophrenic. Where one wing wishes to continue to claim legitimacy by reference to Marxism-Leninism, another, aware that ideological enthusiasm is hard to sustain, argues that social cohesion can be brought by technocratic management resulting in Keynesian-style economic growth.

It is not by any means clear what the future evolution of state socialism will be, but there is something to be said for a rather optimistic scenario.[24] It seems likely that late industrial society depends heavily on scientific knowledge and on willing participation of middle-class skill in every section of the economy. The 'logic' of late industrialism thus increases the institutional importance of that sector of society which has technical rather than ideological competence, and whose way of life benefits from freedom of movement and information. In the final analysis, however, the success of liberalization in the Soviet Union probably depends on what happens in the sphere of state competition. The Soviet Union may no longer be able to afford its historic inefficiencies if it has to compete with the advanced technology produced by the core of capitalist society. Even more important than this is the fact that the ideological cohesion of the socialist bloc has so very clearly ended. The national interest of Russia as compared to China had been dramatically exposed in 1957 when Khrushchev refused to give Mao full details of nuclear weaponry. It is a remarkable and interesting fact, surely ascribable to domestic constraints on American foreign policy-makers, that it took the West more than a decade to adjust their foreign policy accordingly.[25] But this has now been done, and with dramatic consequences: the Soviet Union has been encircled, and may become more so if China is able to use its position with the West – and, perhaps as important, her position close to the most dynamic economies of the contemporary world – to achieve substantial economic growth.

It is useful to pause for a moment in order to highlight the claim being made. The change in the occupational structure of late industrial society, that is, the fact that employment opportunities depend increasingly on higher education, adds massive pressure for a move towards more technical, regularized and softer political rule. Increased pluralism and time make it harder for ideocracies to function as they might like. If these are objective social pressures, it is important to remember that their implementation may or may not be successful. If the entrenched political elite thinks that a demand for softer political rule will spill over into a demand for outright democracy, it will squash liberalization movements. The subtlety demanded of those applying pressure from below will need to be matched by skill on the part of the elites, that is, to strike a balance between giving too much and too little, if liberalization in state socialism is to succeed.

Let us turn to the second type of imitative developmental strategy, that in which various dominant classes and ruling elites, keen to cement themselves in power by controlling the process of modernization, sought by means of 'revolutions from above' to combine capitalism with authoritarianism. Imperial Germany and Imperial Japan showed how economically successful this route to modernity could be, although the traditional elites of China and Russia proved incapable of imitating these examples. This combination is, in numerical terms, the dominant one of our own time.

Barrington Moore has suggested that the combination of capitalism and hierarchy is inherently unstable, that, in other words, it is impossible to conserve a social order by allying oneself to a force as rational and dynamic as capitalism.

> As they proceeded with conservative modernisation, these semi-parliamentary governments tried to preserve as much of the original social structure as they could, fitting large sections into the new building wherever possible. The results had some resemblance to present-day Victorian houses with modern electrical kitchens but insufficient bathrooms and leaky pipes hidden decorously behind newly plastered walls. Ultimately the makeshifts collapsed.[26]

This view is not accepted by every major historical sociologist, and one of them, Michael Mann, has suggested that the stability of the capitalist and hierarchic political economy would be obvious but for the accident of defeat in war.[27] The fact of war *does* make it exceedingly hard to cast light upon Moore's contention, but several considerations suggest that liberalization may be forced on authoritarian capitalist regimes. The pressures at work have just been mentioned. Mann is right to dismisss the radical potential of working classes, but wrong not to realize that a functionally more important middle class comprised of educated labour may soften authoritarian capitalism. It is worth noting that some of these states are less ideocratic than are those inside socialist society, and this may make demands for liberalization that much stronger. Although this is in itself positive, liberalization in the Western world is as perilous and complicated as it is in the Soviet bloc: if demands are too insistent, state elites can be scared and the introduction of softer political rule delayed. In the final analysis, liberalization of such regimes depends heavily on the skill shown by political elites.[28]

If evidence is not available from Imperial Germany and Imperial Japan, it is sensible to turn to other societies of this type. The combination of political hierarchy and capitalism seemed assured in Francoist Spain, but the more the Spanish economy advanced, and thereby became increasingly dependent on educated labour, the more the pressures on authoritarianism mounted. Very interestingly, Spanish capitalists welcomed such liberalization: they had come to realize that accommodation is cheaper than repression.[29] Special circumstances, notably the attractions of the European Community, obscure the Spanish evidence, but it is very striking that NICs like Brazil and Argentina are involved in processes of liberalization that seem to be aided by the state of economic development at which they have now arrived: the supporters of liberalization in Brazil, for example, include the newer middle-class elements of educated labour whose position in the economy is coming to outweigh the influence of old plantation capitalists.[30] This process of liberalization is partly fuelled by the fact that these societies are ones which have a tradition of parliamentary rule that goes back before their relatively late industrialization.[31] But the same forces are at work in rather different contexts. South Korea has witnessed attacks on its repressive authoritarianism; interestingly, these have come from student populations whose importance to the future of society is unquestioned. It may be that the transition to democracy in South Korea will proceed more smoothly than in Latin America. Societal development has gone much further in South Korea than in, say, Brazil; and the presence of a massive economic surplus, rather than powerful pressures from international bankers, may be an important factor allowing for the new regime to be consolidated.

No discussion of such liberalization processes would be complete without stressing that they are likely to be heavily affected by the world political economy. The workings of the world economy are not, as argued, entirely neutral: they reflect the post-war geopolitical settlement. American domination of international institutions has meant fundamental hostility to genuine strengthening – that is, the creation of infrastructural power rather than new waltzes with dictators of the right – of the state in the Third World, except in cases such as that of South Korea where despotism could be ignored on the grounds of anti-communism. Quite as important as the bias of these institutions, however, is the question, currently of great moment, of whether the world economy will continue to allow for growth. Such Third World development as there has been is dependent on the markets of the advanced states, and in particular that of the United States. If the American state decides that the uneven development of capitalism is hurting its national interest so much that protectionism is called for, then the world political economy might again create those instabilities which led in the past to geopolitical conflict. But before considering this possibility, let us first look at the trading nations of the traditional core of capitalist society, not least because their success is playing as important a role as is the growth of the NICs in placing strains on the 'American System'.

Flexible trading and the welfare state

The post-war system of 'embedded liberalism', as we have noted, involved a set of compromises that allowed the Keynesian welfare state to flourish alongside a liberal international economy: the expansion of the international economy went hand in hand with the growth of the modern welfare state. Since the 1970s, however, in a period of slower growth and intensified economic competition, this post-war settlement has been challenged.[32] In this section we examine the strains on the welfare state in an era of intensified international economic competition. Although states have found it more difficult to manage their welfare roles, and many have sought to cut back their social obligations, various advanced international states have found intervention in economic and social arrangement to be central to their success in international markets. High levels of unemployment and economic dislocation have led some to argue that the state's welfare commitments are not compatible with international liberalism; economic malaise has quite generally been attributed to the state's social and economic interventionism.[33] It is certainly clear that a national economy, in a world with greater levels of international trade and financial interdependence, has to be sufficiently competitive to maintain itself inside capitalist society. The particular claim that needs examination here, that of the radical right, is that the competitiveness of a nation depends upon curtailing that combination of domestic Keynesianism and welfare characteristic of the post-war settlement as a whole. Is the welfare state opposed to a successful trading strategy? Does the success of a national capitalism depend upon diminishing the role of the state?

If we contrast two phases of the post-war world we can see how the views of the radical right were generated. The first phase lasted until the late 1960s. It witnessed fabulous economic growth; the productive energies of capitalism allowed a dramatic rise in the standard of living. Furthermore, social citizenship rights were extended: they provided a systematic cushioning to capitalist society and some increase in opportunities for the underprivileged. These were years of social peace. Some thinkers maintained that social cohesion was achieved because the working class had been brainwashed, through consumerism or through indoctrination by an education system. This is highly doubtful. Most working people never actually believed in the virtues of the capitalist ethic; acceptance was pragmatic, based essentially on the capacity of this political economy to provide an ever expanding supply of benefits.[34]

These Keynesian years witnessed capitalism replacing its stick of unemployment with a carrot of growth. Interestingly, Keynes took for granted, much as had Adam Smith and David Hume, that the working class would accept the decisions taken by a liberal and rational elite in order to iron out the troughs and peaks of capitalist development. When growth became harder to achieve in the 1970s, many came to believe that organized groups, notably the working class, freed by citizenship rights from all kinds of deferential behaviour, had become so aggressive that an 'overloaded' state faced a 'rationality crisis' because it had no room to 'steer the system'. The radical right reacted by turning from Keynes to Darwin: it sought to dismantle many citizenship rights and to reintroduce social discipline, largely and probably consciously through extending unemployment. What are we to make of this attempt to dismantle the powers that had accrued to the modern state?

Several considerations lead to extreme suspicion towards these arguments of the radical right. Studies in comparative political economy seem to suggest that the co-operation of labour in most European countries is achieved by some form of corporatism, that is, some arrangement whereby industrial conflict is diminished by integrating the working class, together with major capitalists, in a national economic plan. Corporatism can be more or less restricted, that is, it can apply to some or all of the work-force: the former policy is adopted by Japan and West Germany which integrate workers in large firms but have a vicious labour market for the rest; while the latter is more characteristic of Scandinavia.[35] But in either form, it stands in contrast to the practice of unrestrained collective bargaining which encourages inflation in hard times; it clearly avoids those economic problems resulting from resentment of 'them' as against 'us' which are exacerbated when radical right policies are adopted.[36]

This point can be taken a good deal further by reflecting on the type of work-force needed by late industrial society. The disciplining of a work-force by unemployment may produce something like a nineteenth-century situation: rather unskilled but obedient labour may become available. However, it is surely extremely doubtful whether such labour is the stuff on which late industrialism depends. What is noticeable about Scandinavian social corporatism *and* the micro-corporatism of West Germany and Japan is that the state plays an ever more important role in providing the infrastructure to the economy. One obvious way in which this is true is in the exceptional importance accorded to educational services, the provision of which makes the individualistic tenets of the radical right fantastic. Equally remarkable is the manner in which successful states manage the market in an entirely pragmatic way. In West Germany the state provided seedcorn money to encourage several computer firms, and then allowed the market to decide which was the best: interestingly, this was the exact opposite of the inept way in which the British state handled its computer industry. Similarly, Italian small business was created by the Christian Democratic state through a generous loans policy.[37]

The role of the state in promoting national economic success in an era of slower growth and intensified trade competition is one not fully appreciated by either the right or the left. As we have seen, the attack by the right on the welfare state and economic interventionism ignores the success many states have had in both cushioning and restraining the labour market and promoting industrial adjustment. On the left, proponents of an expanded state presence in industrial planning and ownership have often missed the more important and less obtrusive role that the state can play in promoting growth and adaptation. The expansion of the state sector after the Second World War in Europe, notably in France and Britain, resulted much more from the organizational drives of the state than from market forces *per se*. It appears clear in hindsight that this policy of state-sponsored giantism, which spread so rapidly for reasons of geopolitical competition, was mistaken. The huge nationalized industries of France, for example, have clearly limited the economic policy options of the Mitterrand government.[38] Such large vested interests gained considerable political clout and thereby diminished the autonomy of the state, ate up resources, and made it very hard to respond to international market forces flexibly.[39]

The distinctive combination of state and market that underlies the pheonomenal growth of the Japanese economy is particularly instructive in this regard. The fact that the Japanese state helps her large corporations is well known, but it is only recently that we are beginning to gain some understanding of the manner in which aid is given. It is emphatically not the case that the Japanese state is an all-seeing and absolutely pervasive force, capable of pushing corporations in whatever direction it might wish.[40] Richard Samuels has described the autonomy of business groupings and the limited ability of the Japanese state to control them. The paradox of the situation that results should be familiar here. The state constantly makes large corporations aware of international market forces and points to possible means of adaptation; it does not always get its way, but its process of endless consultation gives it excellent information about business needs. The 'politics of reciprocal consent' show once again that the strength of a state can be great when it respects the autonomy of particular groups and tries to engineer an agreement between them such that autonomous power groupings can contribute to a common purpose.[41]

The lessons that Japan provides for our understanding of the role that states might well seek to play in promoting the performance of the national economy are several. First, direct state ownership and control of industrial production is less effective or important than the attention the state gives to the economic infrastructure. This may involve investing in education, training, or research and development. It may also involve promoting co-operative rather than adversarial labour-management relations.[42] Together these efforts involve what several scholars have called the 'creation of comparative advantage'.[43] The state is involved in creating the conditions for economic growth and industrial adaptation, but it does not exercise direct control. Second, the state works with and often promotes the market. The Japanese state has used the market as a tool of industrial policy, selectively exposing particular industries to international competitive pressures. State officials have used such market openings to encourage the rationalization of a domestic industrial sector; at other times they may wield the threat of opening markets to encourage businesses to comply with other industrial policy goals.[44] Taken together, the capacities of the Japanese state are better understood as nimble fingers rather than heavy hands.

In order to succeed in the international market national societies must organize relations between government and the market with great sophistication. Moreover, the types of relations that are likely to promote economic growth and industrial competitiveness are not easily captured in liberal or statist models of the political economy. Contention surrounds this assertion. The claim of the left in many advanced capitalist countries has been that international capitalism controls everything, that its operations prevent, for example, the extension of socialism in any single country; a corollary of this argument is often the demand that a particular state should exit from the capitalist system. It is important to draw distinctions here. International capitalist society certainly *constrains* what happens in societies belonging to the world market, but it does not *control* all that happens. We can justify this remark in two ways. On the one hand, the failures of the Labour government in Britain in the late 1970s are less to be blamed on the machinations of international bankers than the unfortunate fact that the party had a poor economic policy and no clear idea how to finance its social experiments. On the other hand, international capital still invests in Sweden, despite the *extension* of citizenship rights. Of course, the welfare state can be designed in such a way as not to promote the fortunes of the nation, as can be demonstrated by an examination of one way in which the British and Swedish models of welfare differ. The British system has tended to concentrate on the creation of a welfare safety net, and has had little regard to broader industrial policy. The Swedish situation was completely different, largely because the working class gained self-consciousness – in contrast to the historically antique British working class – at the time of industrialization. A particular policy of great importance in this regard was the provision of mobility allowances in Sweden; this cut labour costs, helped control inflation and thereby allowed Sweden to prosper – no small matter since basic prosperity, rather than a welfare system, remains the key to the life chances of the majority.[45]

This section has limited itself to examining those policies of advanced states within capitalist society which allow them to prosper in the international marketplace. But trading success for even a handful of such nations can cause problems for capitalist society as a whole if the state which provides and maintains the rules for the system as a whole thereby finds its own power increasingly undermined. Has trading success depended upon the background presence of American leadership? Is that leadership now necessarily on the wane? If so, can we expect there to be a turn back from a world open to trade to some version of mercantilism, with all that implies for geopolitical conflict?

The decline and fall of the American empire?

The American system is now widely seen, particularly inside the United States, as being close to collapse. Two challenges to the system are most often cited. First, various capitalist states have, as argued, grown at a much faster rate than has the United States. The most important of these is Japan, whose balance of trade surplus with America reached nearly $60 billion in 1986; significant inroads into American industry have also been made by Europe and by such NICs as Brazil, South Korea and Taiwan. Second, the Third World has mounted a challenge to the liberal ordering of the world economy.[46] Third World countries have learned how to strike better bargains with multinationals, and have nationalized most production of raw materials. Undoubtedly, the most spectacular example of this challenge was that of the oil-price rises pushed through by OPEC. All of this has been taken as evidence, both in academic circles and by the wider public, as evidence of American hegemonic decline. It is well worth noting that sustained belief in the theory would in itself be a political fact of some considerable importance. But before examining the extent to which the theory is likely to be influential, let us first turn to an examination of whether it adequately describes reality.

The theory of hegemonic stability has two key propositions. The first suggests that capitalism fares ill when there is no leading power to provide certain key functions, most notably the provision of an international currency and the opening of world markets. The rivalry between Britain and Germany before the First World War and the power vacuum of the inter-war years lend obvious support to this view. The second proposition, that exercise of hegemony is necessarily self-liquidating, is the one that we need to examine most. The argument often made at this pooint is that the position in which the United States now finds itself is equivalent to that of Britain at the end of the nineteenth century. In Gilpin's words:

> Much as it happened in the latter part of the nineteenth century and the interwar period, the relative decline of the dominant economy and the emergence of new centers of economic power have led to increasing economic conflicts. During such periods of weak international leadership, international economic relations tend to be characterized by a reversion to mercantilism (economic nationalism), intense competition and bargaining among economic powers, and the fragmentation of the liberal interdependent world economy into exclusive blocs, rival nationalisms, and economic alliances.[47]

If this parallel is exact, then there is every reason to believe that the peace of 1945 may *not* be long. If that is so, we may then face that complex interaction of capitalism and states that brought disaster to Europe, and that may now bring disaster to the world.

There are several reasons for scepticism about this. But before outlining them, it is useful to note that there are several theories of the decline of great powers. The essence of hegemonic stability theory is in the claim that, to adapt Jean-Paul Sartre, decline is due to other people. In this view, decline is the result of the hegemonic power providing key services of open markets and defence by itself. Put differently, it provides public goods which others who benefit from them refuse to support financially; these states act as classical free-riders. This is not the way in which the decline of great powers has always been seen. Hegemonic stability makes it necessary to *explain* decline, believing that it is essentially abnormal; in contrast, decline has traditionally been seen as so normal that what would really call for explanation is renewal! Political theorists from Polybius to Montesquieu stressed that decline resulted from arrogant overextension, bringing in its train the disastrous acquisition of territories expensive to control as well as wars on two fronts.[48] Economic theory suggests an alternate view, but one that sees decline as equally normal. To retain riches in a competitive international environment requires constant adaptation. Most societies, however, institutionalize the moment of their success and fail to renew continually their economic dynamism. Such 'errors of police', to use Adam Smith's phrase, are surely historically normal. What sort of explanation for decline help us make sense of the American case?

It is very important indeed to begin by insisting that American power remains very great indeed.[49] Many believed that the closure of the 'gold window' in 1971 meant a radical decline in American power. In fact, power has come to be exercised in a different manner.[50] If, before 1971, America was content to provide certain services, it is now keen, in a rather predatory manner, to reap the benefit of its continuing pre-eminence within the world political econony; increasingly, the United States, even more than its allies, is free-riding on the system it helped create. If, before 1971, the dollar standard enabled it to pass on its inflation, the power of the United States since then has been made brutally evident in its capacity to import, during the Reagan years, most surplus world capital for its own purposes. In so far as this policy has necessitated high American interest rates, it has noticeably added to the debt burden of the developing world; this means that the destiny of much of the Third World, despite much sound and fury, remains largely in the hands of the advanced world. Equally, although the dynamic centres of economic production and wealth have shifted, the United States continues to dominate in key areas of industrial production and in the multinational control of business. It is worth noting here that the British and American parallel fails to note a crucial change in industrial organization. British economic leadership was very quickly undermined because its portfolio investment in the Third World encouraged, indeed *necessitated* autonomous economic growth. In contrast, American investment abroad has been by multinational companies; these companies represent continued structural power in the United States.[51] In underlying 'structures' of production, technology and knowledge, as Susan Strange argues, there has not been a meaningful decline in the American position.[52] Moreover, when military power is brought into consideration, the asymmetries of power within the capitalist core area remain striking. It is these various 'structures' of hegemonic power that others also look to in stressing the continuity in the American position. In this regard, some scholars note that American power has also rested on the projection of a diverse set of cultural and political norms – American ideas, popular culture, language – that are not quickly dislodged by shifts in the economic distribution of power.[53] In these various ways, the notion of hegemony is expanded and thereby enduring continuities of American power are appreciated.

It is very unlikely that agreement can be reached on the exact extent to which America remains a hegemonic power. The current debate between experts on this matter is made inconclusive because of different perceptions: a glass half full for one side seems half empty for the other. It is accordingly helpful if we go beyond narrow matters of measurement, and suggest that the present position of the United States is in no way comparable to that of Britain at the end of the nineteenth century. One cautionary point should be made at the outset. Evidence of decline is partly the result of an optical illusion. The supposed 'golden era' of American hegemony in the early post-war period, on which these trends are based, is often misread. During this earlier period, the United States was already willing to countenance departures from its liberal multilateral vision. In agriculture, shipping, and regional integration, the United States willingly accepted non-liberal economic arrangements.[54] Moreover, even during this period of unprecedented hegemonic power, the United States had systematic problems in using its dominant position to implement its policies across a range of issues. In matters of East–West trade, the integration of Europe, and in negotiations over international trade rules, the United States was less successful than a conventional view of hegemonic power would expect. Economic and political relations among the advanced capitalist countries may currently be a muddle of conflict and co-operation, but this muddle extends back into the early post-war period. When the initial years of American hegemony are properly understood, the trajectory of increasing disarray may not be so steep. The United States was not in its supposed 'golden' past able to have its way in every instance, even if it could at the time of Suez. Not much has changed: the United States may not get its way easily now but, in the last analysis, it still tends to do so on matters it deems of vital interest.

The most important consideration, from which much follows, can be highlighted by simply saying that Britain was never a hegemonic power in the sense that the United States has been. It is true that Britain gained a short period of pre-eminence from being the first industrial nation. But that pre-eminence was necessarily short-lived because of the presence within the European system of states that sought to compete, militarily and economically, with Britain. The position of the United States is quite different from this. The United States faces a geopolitical challenge from *outside* capitalist society and an economic challenge from *within* it. Let us consider both of these in turn.

The geopolitical position of the United States is highly favourable. It is no longer possible to take seriously the notion that the free world is faced by a monolithic challenge from communist society. China and the Soviet Union are competing powers, which is to say that the principle of national sovereignty has here won out over larger social identity. That this is so, of course, masssively weakens the position of the Soviet Union; faced with a war on two fronts, and an economy clearly debilitated by high defence spending, it is clearly a great power in decline. Moreover, it is possible, even probable, that, as argued, there will be, if not an end, then a diminution of ideology in socialist society. In any case, challenges are unlikely to come from the Soviet Union because of very clear and well-established agreements over spheres of influence between, as Raymond Aron felicitously named them, the 'enemy partners'.[55] Similar understandings with China have been achieved; they may prove to be equally sustainable.

The United States has obvious fundamental advantages within capitalist society that it would be naive to overlook. Britain was never able to exercise much seigniorage from the international monetary system, despite the fact that the price of gold before 1914 was largely set in London. France and Germany were genuine rivals, and only held sterling in so far as they felt it in their interest to do so.[56] The allies have behaved quite differently since 1945. Germany supported the dollar at the end of the 1960s, and that role has been taken over in turn by Saudi Arabia and by Japan. The reason for this, and for general tolerance of recent erratic and predatory American behaviour, is simple. The United States has a measure of control over other capitalist nations because it provides defence for capitalist society as a whole. Something of great importance follows from this. Britain's decline was made the more speedy by its being forced to acquire a territorial empire. The fact that the United States has no military rivals within capitalist society means that its empire, or area of hegemony, can in principle remain non-territorial. The point about the Vietnam War in this context is that it was genuinely unnecessary, as many of Britain's imperial involvements were not. It is possible for the United States to withdraw from overexposed positions in the world, an option unavailable to nineteenth-century Britain. Of fundamental importance is the fact that no power in capitalist society seems likely to challenge the United States. The settlement has solved 'the German problem', while there is general awareness that bipolar competition in nuclear weaponry is likely to enhance world security.

There is a still more important recent historical development that distinguishes the British situation from that facing the United States. At the end of the nineteenth century, mercantilist practices were attractive because capitalism at that time could prosper through state planning of markets and of industrial enterprises; according to hegemonic stability theory, such practices should again prove attractive to the hegemon as it loses it competitive edge. Sure enough, there has been some protectionism by the United States, largely through imposing 'voluntary' export quotas. None the less, protectionism is not dominant. The point of our discussion of flexible trading arrangements, whose salience seems to be increasing dramatically, is not that states are likely to withdraw from managing the economy – on the contrary, management will probably take a new form – but that direct industrial planning is less likely to be successful. What seems to matter for economic success is participation in the market, both so as to ensure flexible production and so that key breakthroughs at the frontiers of technology can be appreciated, a development which explains the growth of joint ventures of diverse sorts in areas of high technology. State leaders are reluctant to retreat from the market because these factors are widely appreciated. Such leaders are, moreover, constrained by the impact of domestic political institutions on American trade policy. As Judith Goldstein argues, domestic institutions that are biased in favour of liberal trade have persisted long after adverse international economic conditions might have otherwise propelled a shift to protection. Domestic trade institutions were established at the moments of hegemonic ascendancy and, once in place, are difficult to reform, even when newly injured domestic groups clamour for protection.[57] Behind this argument is a set of claims about the manner in which institutional structures shape and constrain foreign economic policy. Policy is not just the reflexive response to international economic change or the wishes of dominant domestic groups.[58] Hegemonic decline may generate new types of domestic imperative for the United States, but they will be mediated by prevailing institutions that preserve old values and norms. State leaders may further be constrained by the international regimes they established at the end of the war. These, too, manifest a certain political autonomy: regimes may persist and continue to matter as guides to state conduct well after the underlying distribution of power and interests that created them have changed.[59] Investigation of how and in what ways regimes matter continues to be a vital area for inquiry. It seems clear that a proper appreciation of the nature and importance of international regimes requires attention to their interplay with evolving domestic structures and societal interests.[60] In any event, they provide for either an alternative or a supplement to the more rigid predictions contained in the theory of hegemonic decline. Equally importantly, state leaders are subject to pressures from new societal groupings, of multinational bankers and corporations, which have come to realize that their success in the world economy depends upon guaranteeing openness and resisting the protectionist impulse. Even those American firms that are severely injured by imports of goods from abroad often have more complex interests that protection would poorly serve. This complexity of economic interest is driven above all by the extension of trade and the internationalization of production. Even firms that are disadvantaged in domestic markets often have foreign subsidiaries and foreign markets that make protection counterproductive.[61]

The British situation differs from that of the United States in other ways. Most obviously, Britain's precipitate decline resulted from genuine exhaustion brought about as a result of long-term participation in two world wars. The United States rose to power partly because of limited participation in war; the invention of nuclear weapons makes it unlikely that it will be exhausted by war. It is, of course, striking that Vietnam did so very much damage to the American, and thus to the world, economy; but there is no reason to believe that much more damaging military conflicts with key allies will lead to something much worse. But if the decline of Britain was speeded up in this way, it was perhaps inevitable that this decline would be very large indeed. Paul Kennedy has rightly noted that the resource portfolio, that is, the natural endowment and population, of Britain is very small; as a consequence British decline was always likely to be very great. The United States, in contrast, is a continental power with a huge portfolio. If the United States falls to the level of its resource base, as it more or less now has done, it will still unquestionably remain the key player in the international market.[62] As important as its military dominance as a lever over its allies is the potential denial of access to its market, overwhelmingly the largest in the world.

What has been said to this point can be summarized simply: the analogy between Britain at the end of the nineteenth century and the contemporary United States is in significant ways a poor one. Two particular claims have been made, that the United States has not yet declined very significantly and that its situation in the world polity is entirely different, most notably in its having far better geopolitical cards to play. None of this, however, is to deny the fact that there has been some decline in the position of the United States: in 1981 the United States was a net creditor to the world to the tune of $141 billion, but by the end of 1987 it owed the rest of the world something over $400 billion – a rate of borrowing that would lead to total debt equalling current GNP by the end of this century.[63] How should this decline be explained? Our argument here is that similar processes that led to the decline of Britain are at work in the American case, although we do not, as argued, expect decline to go nearly as far. But exactly what are the processes at work?

There is little to recommend hegemonic stability's theory of decline. Britain provided few services for the system as a whole, although there may be something to the notion that the United States was a free-rider on the protection provided by the British navy. But is the United States being exhausted by the provision of defence for its allies and by continuing to keep its markets open in the face of formal and informal protectionism elsewhere?[64] There is some truth to both these claims, but each tends to be exaggerated. Figures that indicate that the United States is being destroyed by high defence expenditures, both absolutely and in comparison to its allies, are very much open to question. Most obviously, defence expenditure, at less than 7 per cent of GNP, is not now historically high, and it is very hard to credit it with causing loss of American competitiveness, especially given the economic success of South Korea and Sweden, both countries which spend as large a proportion of GNP on defence as does the United States. Such figures do not include 'offset' payments from the allies, nor do they include hidden allied costs, notably those of conscription and of the provision of physical assets. A proper accounting would suggest that the major European members of NATO pay nearly as large a share of GNP for defence as does the United States; Japan is the only major power to pay significantly less.[65] Moreover, such figures do not include the informal economic privileges that accrue to the United States, almost as a form of military rent and because of fears that it might close off its huge market;[66] it is this which has led Japan massively to increase its budget for aid, to prop up the dollar and to refrain from developing its own aerospace industry. It is this which leads advanced capitalist states, as noted, to support the dollar, that is, to pay informally for their defence. Equally sceptical points can be made about the claim that decline results because the protectionism of other states is the key to their success. German economic success at the end of the nineteenth century may have been helped by tariff walls, but it was not really ascribable to these to any significant degree; the same seems true of Japan today. An important study by Bergsten and Cline argues that if Japan had no import barriers at all, America's near $50 billion trade deficit with Japan in 1985 would only have been reduced by between $5 billion and $8 billion, and that $5 billion would have been added to that deficit if the United States had removed its own considerable barriers to Japanese imports.[67]

Although they are hard to prove decisively, we find traditional theories of decline far more plausible in explaining both the British and American cases. *Economically*, both Britain and the United States institutionalized the moments of their success, built in each case around a particular set of industries, and failed thereafter to adapt quickly to changed circumstances. This failure can partly be explained in the British case by the possibility of trading, especially in the inter-war years, in protected imperial markets. American failure to adapt has partly been caused by it possessing an option denied smaller trading states: it has often chosen to use its power to change the rule of international norms rather than to make its society flexible enough to compete – an option which seems now to have ever diminishing returns. The point at issue can be summarized by saying that one reason for distrusting the 'decline by service provision' of hegemonic stability theory is that it fails to pay proper attention to the inventiveness, diligence and adaptability of trading states; our argument, in contrast, has been that their success is very largely their own. *Politically*, both Britain and the United States came to suffer from military overextension. This is obvious in the British case, but needs highlighting for the United States. This can best be done by noting that the crises of the American economy have been sudden: they resulted from Vietnam and from the military Keynesianism of Ronald Reagan.

One final consideration is worth reiterating. Britain's over-extension was almost inevitable: as soon as rival powers sought to enter its informal empire, it was forced into territorial acquisitions that were bound in the long run to ruin a very small island state. What is noticeable about the United States, in contrast, is that overextension is not inevitable. The Vietnam débâcle was not in fact necessary for the health of American capitalism.[68] This is to say that the United States has much more room for manoeuvre in the world polity than the grand strategy that it adopted in the 1940s allows. It is indeed slightly surprising that Americans have not realized the immensity of their power. If a Third World country leaves the arena of the world market, it is now apparent that it has to return given that only the West has sufficient capital to ensure development.[69] It is at least *possible*, in other words, for the United States to take visceral, naive and bipolar anti-communism out of its geopolitical grand strategy, and thereby to help arrest that part of its decline caused by overextension.[70]

Conclusion

The American system has great achievements to its name, certainly for the advanced world, including the United States itself, and for at least some parts of the Third World. Its greatest achievement has been peace inside the heartland of capitalist society and between capitalist and socialist systems – although we must reiterate immediately that much of the Third World has been devastated since 1945 by classical and by proxy wars of hideous intensity. This system is now working much less well than previously. This can be seen particularly clearly in international monetary affairs. The refusal of the United States to balance its budget is responsible for fundamental exchange rate instability. This has hit Third World debtor countries particularly hard; it may play a very significant part in undermining the liberalizations currently being tried in Brazil and Argentina.

We do not expect the American system to be suddenly replaced, both because of the structural power of the United States and the fact that no other state wishes to provide international leadership. It is quite likely that this impaired and leaky system will carry on more or less as it is at present constituted – perhaps with more trading within regional blocs but also with increasing participation in the world market of high technology. One can predict that the United States will try to increase military rent from its allies, that this will be successfully achieved, and that it will solve no long-term problems associated with economic decline – although it will ensure that the world economy will not prosper, with all that means for the developing world, as it might. It is possible to imagine a different policy.[71] The United States could enhance its position and that of its allies by sharing decision-making in crucial areas. Easily the most important such area is that of perceptions of geopolitical dangers. The fundamental reason why America's allies do not help more with the burden of defence is that they do not accept the definition of that burden given by the United States: they have a very different view of state socialism and an entirely proper awareness that nationalism and various local dynamics, rather than communism, stand behind most turbulence in the Third World. If the United States learned such lessons from its allies, its burden would be diminished; and the burden for capitalist society as a whole, and not just for an American version of the same, would then be more likely to be generally shared. We doubt that a smaller burden and greater equity in its sharing would in itself cure America's economic decline, but the fact that this excuse for decline had been removed might concentrate attention on the need for education and industrial policies in place of a naive desire to blame others for one's own failure.

The United States is at a turning point, and the grand strategy that guided it for so long is being reassessed. Domestic capitalists are unlikely to stand in the way of the new policy outlined here given the obvious dynamism of the contemporary world market. But McCarthyism made the American elite fearful of electoral punishment for weakness towards communism, and any new policy must be able to show that such punishment is unlikely to be meted out once again. It is important to have international understanding such that no shocks will create such strong domestic popular pressure, as was the case at the end of President Carter's term of office when the Soviet Union invaded Afghanistan. However, domestic pressures can all too easily be exaggerated. Kennedy was able to 'lose' Laos without the American public knowing about it, very largely because the future of that state was not defined in advance as something which would affect American prestige. The same could have happened with Vietnam, perhaps as late as 1965; that it did not is the result far more of mistaken elite policy than of domestic pressure. If the American elite can regain the cohesion that it lost as the result of Vietnam, the intelligent leadership it could offer might well make an historic difference.

6
Conclusions

This book has had two principal themes. First, we have posed the issue of the capacity of states, in various historical epochs, to act on behalf of larger social purposes. What makes the state an efficacious agent of change? Second, we have argued that a proper understanding of the role that the state has played in history needs to draw upon the insights of liberalism, realism and Marxism. We can now offer a systematic review of these issues in turn.

The changing nature of state capacity

A central task of this book has involved gaining a historical appreciation of the nature of state capacity. The notion of state capacity is *not* straightforward: above all it is an error to equate the strength or autonomy of the state with the ability of state elites to ignore other social actors or to impose their will in any simple manner on society. If this were the case, totalitarian states, which seek to suppress the independence of other social actors, would be most capable of realizing state goals and of promoting larger social purposes. Such a conclusion is not justified: a deeper dimension of state power has more to do with the state's ability to work through and with other centres of power. The capacity of states to act rationally is furthered and not curtailed when the state co-ordinates other autonomous power sources. It is this finding that explains why the distinction between the despotic and infrastructural powers of the state has been so useful for our analysis. We have seen that it was the increase in the infrastructural capacities of the state that set the stage for the tremendous growth in the power and wealth of European states as they rose out of their agrarian past; equally, infrastructural power seems to be an ever more crucial element in allowing states to prosper in the contemporary global economy.

A definitive conception of what makes for a capable state is elusive because the specific characteristics and activities of states that promote larger social goals change over time and differ across national experiences. The history of states in the process of industrialization makes this abundantly clear. No single configuration of state and economy captures the necessities of industrial success at every historical juncture. This was Gerschenkron's seminal observation in his study of 'early' and 'late' industrializing countries. The more backward a country entering into industrialization, the more explosive the spur of industrialization and the more concentrated and large-scale the organization of industry, banks, and state bureaucracy. 'So viewed,' Gerschenkron argued, 'the industrial history of Europe appears not as a series of mere repetitions of the "first" industrialization but as an orderly system of graduated deviations from that industrialization.'[1] The roles that states find it necessary to play in economic development vary as widely as do the actual abilities of those states to play such a role.

A further consideration undermines any static notion of state capacity. The circumstances that a state faces will change and so also, therefore, will the specific instruments and activities that are best suited to its purposes. An industrializing state may be said to be strong if it creates a steel industry behind tariff walls; but its continuing strength may best be safeguarded by a determination to keep that industry efficient by removing protection. In this sense the capacity of the state is not only associated with its ability to intervene and shape industrial society, but also in its ability to withdraw or abstain from intervention: this is the 'irony' of state strength.[2] The expansion of the public sector in industrial and developing countries in the post-war period was given impetus as states sought to strengthen the international position of domestic industry.[3] This enlargement of the state's role as manager and producer in such sectors as steel, motor-vehicles and energy was accomplished by states with strong étatist traditions. Well-established and centralized state bureaucracies ensured that industrial development would meet state goals. Yet in later periods the balance of power between the central state and the public enterprises shifted in favour of the latter. State control was undermined as clientelistic relations emerged and direct claims on public revenue enlarged.[4] In many respects, the current interest in privatization and public sector reform in developed and developing countries amounts to an attempt to reconstitute state power. Ironically, by shedding these public responsibilities state officials are seeking to recoup state capacity – which most hope to use in new and more effective ways. The message for this discussion is clear. The power of the state is greatest when the state is able to maximize options at subsequent moments of decision. The ability to act flexibly – to intervene, withdraw, reform or abstain – is at the heart of state capacity.

Normative considerations

Throughout this book we have sought to engage with liberalism, Marxism and realism, for they are the major schools of social theory concerned with the state. We have used these theories as tools to focus on major sets of social and geopolitical relationships. Our references to these social theories, however, have been on an *ad hoc* basis: some theoretical statements have been endorsed, others have been questioned. These concluding remarks present a more system-atic account. Our remarks serve in an obvious sense as a summary of certain positions already taken; but they have a second function. In so far as the future is open, that is, to the extent to which the structural forces at work in our societies allow for genuine options of one sort or another, its character will depend on whether we understand this, and act with wisdom in the light of our knowledge. Hence these comments are largely normative in character; they suggest a style of thought that may increase the rationality of our actions.

Analysis of the state cannot do without realism. In internal affairs, the insistence of realism that a state has become the main means by which to guarantee a settled way of life, and, even more important, the chance of participating in the international market, is entirely meritorious. In contemporary circumstances, this prin-ciple is of especial relevance to Third World countries. There is a relationship between the capacity of a state to mobilise its citizenry and its chances of developing economically. Realism's view of the external behaviour of states remains quite as relevant. States seek security in international society because there is no world order, whether based on a single government or shared norms, that can control or discipline states which threaten to disrupt settled life. Nuclear weapons and the geopolitical settlement of 1945 have created rather stable blocs in the advanced world, but the necessity of rational calculation between these blocs remains as important as ever. Whether careful calculation of means and ends comes to characterize the world polity as a whole is, in an age of nuclear proliferation, one of the key questions facing us.

But realism is a necessary rather than a sufficient condition to understanding the role of the state in the past, as well as to preparing us to think more clearly about the future. One difficulty is that realism has sometimes been, and may again be, prone to naive simplification. This can be particularly so if realism combines with relativist epistemology; it is then argued that our standards of judgement are those of our way of life, that is, our nation, and there is no possibility, and hence desirability, of making universalistic statements of any kind.[5] This is rather abstract but it underlies a crude version of realism according to which states simply seek to increase their own power. This seems hard and practical; in fact it is usually a terrible guide to practice and theory. Clausewitz was somewhat prone to believe in this simplistic version of realism in his youth, but as he grew older he came to realize that the more limited policy of Frederick the Great had, in fact, achieved more than the blind ascension to extremes of his earlier hero, Napoleon.[6] Aron was surely right to draw our attention to Montesquieu's belief that:

> International law is based by nature upon this principle: that the various nations ought to do, in peace, the most good to each other and, in war, the least harm possible, without detriment to their genuine interests.[7]

Realism is most effective, in other words, when it is a universalist doctrine aware of and responsive to the situation of others. The deepest and proper normative implication of realism stresses that the best way to increase security is often through moderation. This advice can be hard to follow when the international system is divided between competing ideological camps; but it is then that the advice is important.

But even if realism can avoid its own errors, it remains true that it has weaknesses. Two very important weaknesses are pointed to by liberalism: they represent in turn the greatest strengths of this major ideological tradition. First, liberalism insists that political power needs to be subject to control, a problem to which realism tends to be rather blind. Stalinism and Nazism demonstrate by themselves the justice of the liberal claim that illiberal regimes can terrorize their own citizens. Second, it is a fact that liberal regimes have a good record of not engaging in war with each other, although it may be that this has been as much the result of luck and geography as of determinate social processes.[8] The actions of liberal states towards each other should correspondingly go beyond the actions of minimal realism towards, when necessary, the attempt to create a league of such nations.

But liberalism has dreadful failings as well, and these are well brought out by considering realism again. Liberalism is prone to oscillate between spinelessness and naive brutality in its relations with non-liberal states. The appeasement of the inter-war years stands as the foremost example of weakness. At that time, liberal states refused to enforce a peace treaty, and simply fed the appetite of a dictator by refusing to stand firm. However, an excessive desire for strength can be, and has been, quite as dangerous. Liberalism is an ideology, and when it is militant it can interpret the world in binary terms, as divided between friends and enemies. If liberalism can be good to its friends, the harshness with which it treats its enemies can be quite opposed to the dictum of Montesquieu. Strength may be needed, but nothing in international politics is gained by refusing to accept the baseline presumption that other states have the right to exist. The United States has been particularly naive in this manner in its dealings with the Soviet Union and with those Third World states whose attempt to enhance state power for developmental purposes deserves understanding, acceptance and a realization that policies might be designed to encourage the eventual liberalization of such regimes. This criticism should not be misunderstood. On occasion, American geopolitical thinkers have suggested that the naive views of the people prevent the conduct of a traditional geopolitical strategy by a rational elite – the implication being that democratic control of foreign policy is an obstacle and a nuisance.[9] No regime is perfect, and we have seen that liberal regimes can suffer from shortsighted popular enthusiasm. But elitist criticisms of democracy often fail to realize that such behaviour is itself often reactive to political styles which fail to trust the people. Moreover, governments of the advanced societies usually have the capacity, if they act skilfully, to engineer consent; the 'people' may well respond to demands placed upon them if they are told the truth. In so far as democracy presents difficulties for a foreign policy elite, it is at least in part the result of popular misperceptions that have been caused by previous governmental information. The people may well have the capacity for long-term calculation if they are treated as politically consenting adults. In any case, one needs always to compare dangers. Probably the greatest danger, especially in the nuclear age, is that an elite retains unrestrained warmaking capacity. In this context, it is entirely proper to remember that the American people were perfectly prepared to fight in the 'good' war of 1941–5, and that they, rather than the experts, were right to refuse to continue the war in Vietnam. A good case can indeed be made to support the contention that the greatest blunders in recent American foreign policy owe more to the failings of the elite than to insistent and naive pressures of the people. Democratic control of foreign policy is ultimately, in other words, a positive resource because of its capacity to weed out poor policies.

Much that has been said to this point can be summarized as a call for calculation, and sometimes for restraint. The hopes that can be entertained for the future depend, as much internally as externally, on the ability of states to become more rational. This is to go absolutely against Marxism's fundamental hope of replacing states with a transnational society of classes.[10] The creation of a socialist world would probably destroy us all, although the fact that class conflict has become very firmly established *within* states makes it most unlikely that this will actually happen. But these critical comments cannot detract from the one point of Marxism which must remain at the centre of attention. States live inside capitalist society. As the dynamic centre of capitalism moves from one place to another, so states themselves rise and fall. In the past, state elites were not able to adjust their fortunes to changes in circumstance with sufficient skill to prevent massive wars. It remains to be seen whether they can manage better in the contemporary world.

Notes

Chapter 1

1 We have in mind here particularly the works of Nicos Poulantzas and the German 'Capital Logic' School. For the former, see especially Poulantzas, *Political Power and Social Classes* (London: New Left Books, 1973); and *State, Power, Socialism* (London: New Left Books, 1978), as well as the critical commentary in B. Jessop, *Nicos Poulantzas* (London: Macmillan, 1985); exemplars of the work of the latter school are contained in J. Holloway and S. Picciotto, eds, *State and Capital* (London: Edward Arnold, 1978).

2 This definition draws on and expands that given by M. Mann, 'The Autonomous Power of the State: Its Origins, Mechanisms and Results' in J. A. Hall, ed., *States in History* (Oxford: Basil Blackwell, 1986). Our understanding of the state is influenced by M. Weber, *Economy and Society* (New York: Bedminster Press, 1968), Vol. 2, Chapter 9 and Vol. 3, Chapters 10 and 13.

3 M. Mann, *Sources of Social Power. Vol. I: A History of Power from the Beginning to 1760 AD* (Cambridge: Cambridge University Press, 1986), Chapter 10.

4 The term 'stateness' comes from J. P. Nettl, 'The State as a Conceptual Variable', *World Politics*, vol. 20 (1968).

5 J. A. Hall, 'Theory' in M. Haralambos, ed., *Developments in Sociology, Vol. 2* (Ormskirk: Causeway Press, 1986).

6 A. Arblaster, *The Rise and Decline of Western Liberalism* (Oxford: Basil Blackwell, 1984); J. A. Hall, *Liberalism* (London: Paladin, 1988).

7 For a commentary on Smith's argument, see D. Winch, *Adam Smith's Politics* (Cambridge: Cambridge University Press, 1978).

8 A. Hirschman, *The Passions and the Interests* (Princeton, NJ: Princeton University Press, 1977).

9 D. Stewart, 'Account of the Life and Writings of Adam Smith, LL.D.' in A. Smith, *Essays on Philosophical Studies* (Oxford: Oxford University Press, 1980), p. 322.

10 In this connection, it is worth remembering that *The Wealth of Nations* is a 'handbook for legislators' designed to show them the need to make the market work properly. Cf. N. Phillipson, 'Adam Smith as Civic Moralist' in I. Hont and M. Ignatieff, eds, *Wealth and Virtue* (Cambridge: Cambridge University Press, 1983).

11 Stewart, 'Life and Writings of Adam Smith', p. 313.

12 I. Kant, 'Perpetual Peace' in C. J. Friedrich, ed., *The Philosophy of Kant* (New York: Modern Library, 1949). Cf. M. Doyle, 'Kant, Liberal Legacies and Foreign Affairs', *Philosophy and Public Affairs*, Vol. 12, nos 3 and 4 (1983); and P. Q. Hirst, 'Peace and Political Theory', unpublished paper (1986).

13 R. Cobden, *Political Writings*, Vol. 2, p. 377, cited in A. J. P. Taylor, *The Troublemakers* (London: Paladin, 1969), p. 49.

14 J. A. Hobson, *Imperialism* (London: James Nisbet, 1902), p. 51.

15 This view was expressed most forcefully in 1848 in *The Manifesto of the Communist Party*; this is reprinted in *The Marx–Engels Reader*, ed. R. C. Tucker (New York: Norton, 1972).

16 Modern Marxists, perhaps most notably Poulantzas, seeking to allow for some 'relative autonomy of the state', have drawn heavily on this argument of Marx's. See also R. Miliband, *The State in Capitalist Society* (New York: Basic Books, 1969); P. Anderson, *Lineages of the Absolutist State* (London: New Left Books, 1974); G. Therborn, *What Does the Ruling Class Do When it Rules?* (London: New Left Books, 1978); and C. Offe, 'Structural Problems of the Capitalist State', *German Political Studies*, Vol. 1 (1974). A useful overview is M. Carnoy, *The State and Political Theory* (Princeton, NJ: Princeton University Press, 1984).

17 A. O. Hirschman, *Essays in Tresspassing* (Cambridge: Cambridge University Press, 1981).

18 W. B. Gallie, *Philosophers of War and Peace* (Cambridge: Cambridge University Press, 1978).

19 Notably in V. I. Lenin, *Imperialism, the Highest Stage of Capitalism* (New York: International Publishers, 1939).

20 R. Gilpin, *The Political Economic of International Relations* (Princeton, NJ: Princeton University Press, 1987), Chapters 1 and 2.

21 There is a very large literature that makes this claim. A. G. Frank's *Capitalism and Underdevelopment in Latin America* (New York: Monthly Review, 1967) makes the claim forcefully for the modern Latin American case, while I. Wallerstein's *The Modern World System* (New York: Academic Press, 1974) makes use of the analytic insights in order to explain historical development.

22 K. Thomas, 'Social Origins of Hobbes's Political Thought', in K. C. Brown, ed., *Hobbes Studies* (Cambridge, MA: Harvard University Press, 1965).

23 S. Huntingdon, *Political Order in Changing Societies* (New Haven, CT: Yale University Press, 1968).

24 A. Gerschenkron, *Economic Backwardness in Historical Perspective* (Cambridge, MA: Harvard University Press, 1962).

25 T. Hobbes, *Leviathan*, Part One, Chapter 13, cited in R. Aron, 'La guerre est une caméléon', *Contrepoint*, Vol. 15 (1974).

26 R. Keohane, 'Realism, Neorealism and the Study of World Politics' in Keohane, ed., *Neorealism and its Critics* (New York: Columbia University Press, 1986). Cf. R. Gilpin, 'The Richness of the Tradition of Political Realism' in the same volume.

27 P. Kennedy, *The Rise and Fall of British Naval Mastery* (London: Allen Lane, 1976), Chapter 7.

28 See W. E. Minchinton, ed., *Mercantilism* (Lexington, MA: D. C. Heath, 1969).

29 G. Sen, *The Military Origins of Industrialisation and International Trade Rivalry* (London: Frances Pinter, 1984).

30 The earliest statement of this thesis was C. Kindleberger, *The World in Depression, 1919–1933* (Berkeley: University of California Press, 1973). The fullest working out of this general position is R. Gilpin, *War and Change in World Politics* (Cambridge: Cambridge University Press, 1981).

31 G. Kennan, *American Diplomacy, 1900–1950* (Chicago: University of Chicago Press, 1951).

32 For a discussion of 'strong' and 'weak' states see G. J. Ikenberry, 'The Irony of State Strength: Comparative Responses to the Oil Shocks in the 1970s', *International Organization*, Vol. 40 (1986); and J. A. Hall, 'States and Economic Development: Reflections on Adam Smith' in Hall, *States in History*. A good discussion of 'state capacity' is that of T. Skocpol and K. Finegold, 'State Capacity and Economic Intervention in the Early New Deal', *Political Science Quarterly*, Vol. 97 (1982).

33 S. Strange, 'Supranationals and the State' in Hall, *States in History*. See also P. B. Evans, 'Transnational Linkages and the Economic Role of the State: An Analysis of Developing and Industrialized Nations in the Post-World War II Period' in P. B. Evans, D. Rueschemeyer, and T. Skocpol, eds, *Bringing the State Back In* (New York: Cambridge University Press, 1985).

34 Ikenberry, 'The Irony of State Strength' and *Reasons of State* (Ithaca, NY: Cornell University Press, 1988), Chapter 8. Cf. E. Suleiman, *Private Power and Centralization in France* (Princeton, NJ: Princeton University Press, 1988).

35 T. McDaniel, *Autocracy, Capitalism and Revolution in Russia* (Berkeley: University of California Press, 1988), Chapter 1.

36 Cf. M. Olson, *The Rise and Decline of Nations* (New Haven, CT: Yale University Press, 1982).

37 A. de Tocqueville, *Democracy in America* (New York: Vintage Books, 1945); and *The Old Regime and the French Revolution* (New

York: Anchor Books, 1955). Cf. T. Skocpol, *States and Social Revolution* (Cambridge: Cambridge University Press, 1979).
38 G. J. Ikenberry, 'The State and Strategies of International Adjustment', *World Politics*, Vol. 39 (1986).

Chapter 2

1 The classic statement is that of John Locke, *Two Treatises on Government*, 2nd edn, ed. P. Laslett (Cambridge: Cambridge University Press, 1987). For a magnificent analysis of the genesis of Locke's argument, see R. Ashcraft, *Revolutionary Politics and Locke's Two Treatises on Government* (Princeton, NJ: Princeton University Press, 1986).
2 The clearest statements are those of F. Oppenheimer, *The State* (New York: Free Life Editions, 1975), and W. Eberhard, *Conquerors and Rulers* (Leiden: Brill, 1965). For a commentary, see L. Krader, *Formation of the State* (Englewood Cliffs, NJ: Prentice-Hall, 1968).
3 P. Crone, 'The Tribe and the State', in J. A. Hall, ed., *States in History* (Oxford: Basil Blackwell, 1986), p. 67. Cf. H. Claessen and P. Skalnik, eds, *The Early State* (The Hague: Mouton, 1978).
4 M. Sahlins, *Stone Age Economics* (London: Tavistock, 1974).
5 L. Binford, *In Pursuit of the Past* (London: Thames and Hudson, 1983), Chapter 8.
6 See R. L. Carneiro, 'A Theory of the Origin of the State', *Science*, Vol. 169 (1970).
7 C. Gamble, 'Hunter-Gatherers and the Origins of States' in Hall, *States in History*.
8 See especially E. R. Service, *The Origins of the State and Civilization*, (New York: Norton, 1975).
9 P. Clastres, *Society Against the State* (New York: Basil Blackwell, 1977).
10 M. Mann, *Sources of Social Power: Vol. I: A History of Power from the Beginning to 1760 AD* (Cambridge: Cambridge University Press, 1988), Chapter 2.
11 Crone, 'The Tribe and the State'.
12 Ibid., pp. 65–6.
13 Ibid., p. 68.
14 There are exceptions to this rule. The Vikings who settled Iceland knew the state at home, disliked it, and so created institutions in their 'new land' to avoid it. Medieval Iceland managed without a state for over three centuries; but this society was addicted to feuds, and very far from being an arcadian affair. On this see J. Byock, *Medieval Iceland* (Berkeley: University of California Press, 1988). A similar desire to limit, albeit not to abolish, state power can be seen in the founding of new societies, notably the colonies in North America. On this whole

question, see L. Hartz, *The Liberal Tradition in America* (New York: Harcourt, Brace, 1955); and *idem*, ed, *The Founding of New Societies* (New York: Harcourt, Brace & World 1964).

15 Cf. E. Gellner, *Plough, Sword and Book* (London: Collins, 1988).

Chapter 3

1 D. W. Engel, *Alexander the Great and the Logistics of the Macedonian Army* (Berkeley: University of California Press, 1978). In this section we are generally indebted to P. Crone, *Pre-Industrial Societies* (Oxford: Basil Blackwell, 1989).

2 Cf. J. A. Hall, *Powers and Liberties* (London: Penguin, 1986), Part One.

3 This was the argument of M. Weber, *The Religion of China* (New York: Free Press, 1964).

4 R. Huang, *1587* (New Haven, CT: Yale University Press, 1981), Chapter 2.

5 K. A. Wittfogel, *Oriental Despotism* (New Haven, CT: Yale University Press, 1957). This thesis has been much criticized; see, for instance, E. Leach, 'Hydraulic Society in Ceylon', *Past and Present*, no. 15 (1959); and M. Elvin, 'On Water Control and Management during the Ming and Ch'ing Periods', *Ch'ing-shih wen-t'i*, Vol. 3 (1975).

6 W. Rodinski, *The Walled Kingdom* (London: Fontana, 1984), p. 78.

7 M. Elvin, *The Pattern of the Chinese Past* (California: Stanford University Press, 1973), Chapter 14.

8 Ibid., pp. 318–19.

9 M. Mann, *The Sources of Social Power. Vol. 1: A History of Power from the Beginning to 1760 AD* (Cambridge: Cambridge University Press, 1986), Chapters 10 and 11.

10 I. Karve, *Hindu Society: An Interpretation* (Poona: Deccan College, 1961), p. 40.

11 B. Stein, 'The State and the Agrarian Order' in Stein, ed., *Essays on South India* (New Delhi: Vikas, 1976), p. 86.

12 J. H. Hutton, *Caste in India* (Cambridge: Cambridge University Press, 1946), pp. 123–4.

13 B. Stein, 'The Economic Function of a Medieval South Indian Temple', *Journal of Asian Studies*, Vol. 19 (1960).

14 M. Cook and P. Crone, *Hagarism* (Cambridge: Cambridge University Press, 1977).

15 P. Crone, *Slaves on Horses* (Cambridge: Cambridge University Press, 1980).

16 Ibn Khaldun, *Muqaddimah* (Princeton, NJ: Princeton University Press, 1967). Cf. E. Gellner, *Muslim Society* (Cambridge: Cambridge University Press, 1981).

17 M. Hodgson, *The Venture of Islam* (Chicago: University of Chicago Press, 1974), Vol. 2, p. 105. Cf. C. Cahen, 'Economy, Society, Institutions' in P. M. Holt, A. S. Lambton and B. Lewis, eds, *The Cambridge History of Islam. Vol. I: The Farther Islamic Lands. Islam, Society and Civilisation* (Cambridge: Cambridge University Press, 1970).

18 I. M. Lapidus, *Muslim Cities in the Later Middle Ages* (Cambridge, MA: Harvard University Press, 1967).

19 Hodgson, *The Venture of Islam*, Vol. 2, pp. 355–6.

20 M. Mann, *Sources of Social Power*, Chapters 10 and 12. G. Duby, *The Early Growth of the European Economy* (London: Weidenfeld and Nicolson, 1974); M. M. Postan, *Medieval Economy and Society* (London: Penguin, 1975); and C. Cipolla, *Before the Industrial Revolution* (London: Methuen, 1976).

21 C. Tilly, 'Reflections on the History of European State-Making' in *idem*, ed., *The Formation of National States in Western Europe* (Princeton, NJ: Princeton University Press, 1975), p. 18.

22 J. Goody, *The Development of the Family and Marriage in Europe* (Cambridge: Cambridge University Press, 1983). Cf. E. Todd, *The Causes of Progress* (Oxford: Basil Blackwell, 1987).

23 P. Burke, 'City States' in J. A. Hall, ed., *States in History* (Oxford: Basil Blackwell, 1986).

24 J. H. Myers, *Parliaments and Estates in Europe to 1789* (London: Thames and Hudson, 1975); G. Poggi, *The Development of the Modern State* (London: Hutchinson, 1978).

25 Tilly, 'Reflections on the History of European State-Making' pp. 21–5.

26 E. L. Jones, *The European Miracle* (Cambridge: Cambridge University Press, 1981), Chapter 7.

27 See G. J. Ikenberry, 'The Spread of Norms in the International System', unpublished paper, 1987.

28 C. Tilly, 'Warmaking and Statemaking as Organized Crime' in P. B. Evans, D. Rueschemeyer, and T. Skocpol, eds, *Bringing the State Back In* (New York: Cambridge University Press, 1985), p. 172.

29 Cf. A. Hirschman's notion of 'movable wealth' in 'Exit, Voice, and the State', *World Politics*, Vol. 31 (1978); and B. G. Haskel, 'Access to Society: A Neglected Dimension of Power', *International Organization*, Vol. 34 (1980).

30 D. C. North has spelled out this fundamental double-edged relationship between state and capital, presenting an elaborate utility-maximizing model. See North, *Structure and Change in Economic History* (New York: Norton, 1981). See also M. Levi, 'The Predatory Theory of Rule', *Politics and Society*, Vol. 10 (1981); and J. A. C. Conybeare, 'The Rent-Seeking State and Revenue Diversification', *World Politics*, Vol. 35 (1982).

31 W. H. McNeill, *The Pursuit of Power* (Oxford: Basil Blackwell, 1982), Chapter 1.
32 Ibid., pp. 138–9.

Chapter 4

1 R. Dahrendorf, *Class and Class Conflict in Industrial Society* (London: Routledge and Kegan Paul, 1959).

2 E. Halévy, *A History of the English People in the Nineteenth Century. Vol. I: England in 1815* (London: Benn, 1971).

3 D. Geary, *European Labour Protest, 1848–1945* (London: Methuen, 1984), p. 60.

4 I. Katznelson, *City Trenches* (New York: Pantheon Books, 1981), p. 19.

5 M. Shefter, 'Trade Unions and Political Machines: The Organization and Disorganization of the American Working Class in the Late Nineteenth Century' in I. Katznelson and A. Zolberg, eds, *Working-Class Formation* (Princeton, NJ: Princeton University Press, 1986), p. 197.

6 I. Katznelson, *Black Men, White Cities* (New York: Oxford University Press, 1973), p. 87; also, *idem, City Trenches*, Chapter 3.

7 M. Mann, 'Citizenship and Ruling Class Strategies', *Sociology*, Vol. 21, 1987, p. 342.

8 See T. Skocpol and G. J. Ikenberry, 'The Political Formation of the American Welfare State in Comparative and Historical Perspective', *Comparative Social Research*, Vol. 6 (1983); A. S. Orloff and T. Skocpol, 'Why Not Equal Protection? Explaining the Politics of Public Social Spending in Britain, 1900–1911, and the United States, 1880s–1920', *American Sociological Review*, Vol. 49 (1984).

9 See I. Katznelson, 'Working-Class Formation: Constructing Cases and Comparisons' in Katznelson and Zolberg, *Working-Class Formation* pp. 37–8.

10 See S. Skowronek, *Building a New American State* (New York: Cambridge University Press, 1982).

11 W. Sombart, *Why Is There No Socialism in the United States?* (White Plains, NY: M. E. Sharpe, 1976).

12 Mann, 'Citizenship and Ruling Class Strategies'. See also A. R. Zolberg, 'How Many Exceptionalisms?' in Katznelson and Zolberg, *Working-Class Formation* esp. pp. 399–400.

13 L. Hartz, *The Liberal Tradition in America* (New York: Harcourt, Brace, 1955). See also C. Waisman, *Reversal of Development in Argentina* (Princeton, NJ: Princeton University Press, 1987).

14 B. Moore, *Social Origins of Dictatorship and Democracy* (Boston: Beacon, 1969), p. 444.

15 R. McKibbin, 'Why Was There no Marxism in Great Britain?', *English Historical Review*, Vol. 100 (1984).

16 R. McKibbin, *The Evolution of the Labour Party, 1910–24* (Oxford: Oxford University Press, 1974).

17 T. McDaniel, *Autocracy, Capitalism and Revolution in Russia* (Berkeley: University of California Press, 1988).

18 V. Bonnell, *Roots of Rebellion: Workers' Politics and Organisations in St Petersburg and Moscow, 1900–14* (Berkeley: University of California Press, 1984): McDaniel, *Autocracy, Capitalism and Revolution in Russia.*

19 McDaniel, *Autocracy, Capitalism and Revolution in Russia*, Chapter 1.

20 A. J. P. Taylor, *Bismarck* (New York: Vintage Books, 1967); H. Kissinger, 'The White Revolutionary: Reflections on Bismarck', *Daedalus*, Vol. 95 (1968).

21 One such author is H. U. Wehler, *The German Empire, 1871–1918* (Leamington Spa, Berg, 1984).

22 R. Kaiser, 'Germany and the Origins of the First World War', *Journal of Modern History*, Vol. 55 (1983).

23 Mann, 'Citizenship and Ruling Class Strategies'.

24 N. Angell, *The Great Illusion* 3rd edn (London: George Allen & Unwin, 1911), cited in J. Joll, *The Origins of the First World War* (London: Longman 1984), p. 137.

25 Joll, *The Origins of the First World War*, pp. 126–7.

26 Ibid., p. 136.

27 Ibid., p. 138.

28 R. Robinson, *The Rise, Decline and Revival of the British Empire* (Cambridge: Cambridge University Press, 1984); cf. M. Doyle, *Empires* (Ithaca, NY: Cornell University Press, 1986).

29 R. Aron, *Imperialism and Colonialism* (Leeds: Leeds University Press, 1959).

30 L. Davis and R. A. Huttenback, *Mammon and the Pursuit of Empire* (New York: Cambridge University Press, 1986).

31 W. Sombart, *Händler und Helden* (Munich and Leipzig: Duncker & Humblot, 1915).

32 See E. M. Earle, 'Adam Smith, Alexander Hamilton, Friedrich List: The Economic Foundations of Military Power' in Earle, ed., *Makers of Modern Strategy: Military Thought from Macchiavelli to Hitler* (Princeton, NJ: Princeton University Press, 1971).

33 G. Sen, *The Military Origins of Industrialisation and International Trade Rivalry* (Frances Pinter: London, 1984).

34 D. Lake, *Power, Protection and Free Trade: International Sources of U.S. Commerical Strategy, 1887–1939* (Ithaca, NY: Cornell University Press, 1988). Cf. R. Keohane, 'Reciprocity in International Relations', *International Organization*, Vol. 40 (1986).

35 J. Gallagher and R. Robinson, 'The Imperialism of Free Trade', *Economic History Review*, Vol. 6 (1953).

36 S. F. Cohen, *Bukharin and the Russian Revolution* (Oxford: Oxford University Press, 1980).

37 J. Herf, *Reactionary Modernism* (Cambridge: Cambridge University Press, 1984); J. P. Stern, *Hitler, the Führer and the People* (London: Fontana, 1974).

38 L. Schapiro, *Totalitarianism* (New York: Praeger, 1972).

39 E. H. Carr, *The Twenty Years' Crisis* (London: Macmillan, 1951).

40 J. M. Keynes, *The Economic Consequences of the Peace* (London: Macmillan, 1919).

41 M. Howard, *War and the Liberal Conscience* (Oxford: Oxford University Press, 1978); A. J. P. Taylor, *The Troublemakers* (London: Panther, 1969).

42 N. Angell, *After All* (London: Hamish Hamilton, 1951), cited in Howard, *War and the Liberal Conscience*, p. 107.

Chapter 5

1 For systematic accounts of these monetary negotiations, see R. Gardner, *Sterling–Dollar Diplomacy* (New York: McGraw-Hill, 1969); and A. Van Doermal, *Bretton Woods* (London: Macmillan, 1978).

2 For a summary of differences in American and British understandings of Bretton Woods, see Gardner, *Sterling–Dollar Diplomacy*, pp. 143–4.

3 J. G. Ruggie, 'International Regimes, Transactions, and Change: Embedded Liberalism in the Postwar Economic Order', *International Organization*, Vol. 36 (1982), p. 393.

4 See Gardner, *Sterling–Dollar Diplomacy* pp. 30–5.

5 See J. E. Miller, *The United States and Italy, 1940–80* (Chapel Hill: University of North Carolina Press, 1988) for a good case study.

6 C. Maier, *In Search of Stability* (New York: Cambridge University Press, 1987).

7 J. Frieden, 'Sectoral Conflict and U.S. Foreign Economic Policy, 1914–1940', *International Organization*, Vol. 41 (1988). We have benefited greatly from seeing unpublished work on this period by William Domhoff.

8 J. L. Gaddis, *The United States and the Origins of the Cold War, 1941–7* (New York: Columbia University Press, 1972).

9 S. Hoffmann, *Janus and Minerva* (Boulder, CO: Westview Press, 1987).

10 G. Lundestad, 'Empire by Limitation? The United States and Western Europe, 1945–52', *Journal of Peace Research*, Vol. 23 (1986).

11 J. L. Gaddis, *Strategies of Containment* (New York: Oxford University Press, 1982).

12 E. Gellner, 'Democracy and Industrialisation', *European Journal of Sociology*, Vol. 8 (1967).

13 B. Moore, *Social Origins of Dictatorship and Democracy* (Boston: Beacon Press, 1969).

14 E. Gellner, *Nations and Nationalism* (Oxford: Basil Blackwell, 1983).

15 Those who stress the positive role of authoritarianism on economic development include I. Adelman and C. Morris, *Society, Politics, and Economic Development* (Baltimore, MD: Johns Hopkins University Press, 1967); S. Huntington and J. Dominguez, 'Political Development' in F. Greenstein and N. Polsby, eds, *Handbook of Political Science, Vol. 3* (Reading, MA: Addison-Wesley, 1975); and R. Marsh, 'Does Democracy Hinder Economic Development in the Latecomer Developing Nations?', *Comparative Social Research*, vol. 2 (1979). Those who make the opposite argument include G. William Dick, 'Authoritarian versus Nonauthoritarian Approaches to Economic Development', *Journal of Political Economy*, Vol. 82 (1974); and A. Kohli, 'Democracy and Development' in J. P. Lewis and V. Kallab, eds, *Development Strategies Reconsidered* (Washington, DC: Overseas Development Council, 1987).

16 A classic statement of this position was A. G. Frank, 'The Sociology of Development and the Underdevelopment of Sociology' in *idem, Latin America: Underdevelopment or Revolution* (New York: Monthly Review Press, 1969).

17 P. Evans, *Dependent Development* (Princeton, NJ: Princeton University Press, 1978); G. Gereffi, *The Pharmaceutical Industry and Dependency in the Third World* (Princeton, NJ: Princeton University Press, 1983).

18 S. Haggard, 'The Newly Industrializing Countries in the International System', *World Politics*, Vol. 38 (1986).

19 R. P. Dore, 'Talent and the Social Order in Tokugawa Japan' in J. W. Hall and M. E. Jensen, eds, *Studies in the Institutional History of Early Modern Japan* (Princeton, NJ: Princeton University Press, 1968). Cf. A. O. Hirschman, *Exit, Voice and Loyalty* (Princeton, NJ: Princeton University Press, 1970).

20 J. Brooke, 'Africa Has an Arms Control Problem', *New York Times*, 17 March 1987.

21 H. Lever and C. Huhne, *Debt and Danger* (Harmondsworth: Penguin, 1985); S. Strange, *Casino Capitalism* (Oxford: Basil Blackwell, 1986).

22 G. White and R. Wade, eds, *Developmental States in East Asia* (Brighton: Institute for Development Studies, 1984); F. C. Deyo, ed., *The Political Economy of the New Asian Industrialism* (Ithaca, NY: Cornell University Press, 1987).

23 S. D. Krasner, *Structural Conflict* (Berkeley: University of California Press, 1985).

24 Cf. E. Gellner, 'From the Revolution to Liberalisation', *Government*

and Opposition, Vol. 11 (1976). A revealing and high-powered exchange over this thesis occurred between R. Aron, 'On Liberalisation' and E. Gellner, 'Plaidoyer pour une libéralisation manquée' both in *Government and Opposition*, Vol. 14 (1979).

25 J. L. Gaddis, 'Dividing Adversaries: The United States and International Communism, 1945–58' in *idem, The Long Peace* (New York: Oxford University Press, 1987).

26 Moore, *Social Origins*, p. 438.

27 M. Mann, 'Citizenship and Ruling Class Strategies', *Sociology*, Vol. 21 (1987).

28 G. O'Donnell, P. Schmitter and L. Whitehead, eds, *Transitions from Authoritarian Rule* (Baltimore, MD: Johns Hopkins Press, 1986).

29 S. Giner and E. Sevilla, 'From Despotism to Parliamentarism: Class Domination and Political Order in the Spanish State' in R. Scase, ed., *The State in Western Europe* (London: Croom Helm, 1978).

30 J. G. Merquior, 'Power and Identity: Politics and Ideology in Latin America', *Government and Opposition*, Vol. 19 (1984).

31 N. Mouzelis, *The Politics of the Semi-Periphery* (London: Macmillan, 1986).

32 See R. Keohane, 'The World Political Economy and the Crisis of Embedded Liberalism' in J. H. Goldthorpe, ed., *Order and Conflict in Contemporary Capitalism* (Oxford: Oxford University Press, 1984).

33 For an overview of these attacks on liberal trade policy, see M. Kahler, 'European Protectionism in Theory and Practice', *World Politics*, Vol. 37 (1985).

34 C. Maier, 'The Politics of Productivity: Foundations of American International Economic Policy after World War II' in *idem, In Search of Stability*; A. Wolfe, *The Rise and Fall of the Politics of Growth* (New York: Pantheon Books, 1981).

35 J. H. Goldthorpe, 'The End of Convergence: Corporatist and Dualist Tendencies in Modern Western Societies' in *idem, Order and Conflict in Western European Capitalism*.

36 See C. Crouch, 'Conditions of Trade Union Wage Restraint' in L. N. Lindberg and C. Maier, eds, *The Politics of Inflation and Economic Stagnation* (Washington, DC: The Brookings Institution, 1985).

37 L. Weiss, *Creating Capitalism* (Oxford: Basil Blackwell, 1988).

38 E. Suleiman, *Private Power and Centralization in France* (Princeton, NJ: Princeton University Press, 1988). See also J. Hayward, *The State and the Market* (Brighton: Wheatsheaf Books, 1986); H. B. Feigenbaum, *The Politics of Public Enterprise* (Princeton, NJ: Princeton University Press, 1985); Weiss, *Creating Capitalism*.

39 G. J. Ikenberry, 'The Irony of State Strength: Comparative Responses to the Oil Shocks in the 1970s', *International Organization*, Vol. 40 (1986).

40 See the new interpretation of Japanese state capacities in R. J. Samuels,

The Business of the Japanese State (Ithaca, NY: Cornell University Press, 1987); and D. Friedman, *The Misunderstood Miracle* (Ithaca, NY: Cornell University Press, 1988). The distinctive symbiotic relations between the Japanese state and economy – what he calls 'organized capitalism' – are also discussed by R. Dore in *Flexible Rigidities* (Stanford, CA: Stanford University Press, 1986).

41 Samuels, *The Business of the Japanese State*.

42 See C. Johnson, 'The Japanese Political Economy: A Crisis in Theory' *Ethics and International Affairs*, Vol. 2 (1988).

43 L. Tyson and J. Zysman, 'American Industry in International Competition' in Zysman and Tyson, eds, *American Industry in International Competition* (Ithaca, NY: Cornell University Press, 1983).

44 D. Okimoto, *Betwen MITI and the Market* (Stanford, CA: Stanford University Press, 1988).

45 See P. J. Katzenstein, *Small States in World Markets* (Ithaca, NY: Cornell University Press, 1985).

46 Krasner, *Structural Conflict*.

47 R. Gilpin, 'Economic Interdependence and National Security in Historical Perspective' in K. Knorr and F. N. Trager, eds, *Economic Issues and National Security* (Lawrence: Regents Press of Kansas, 1977), p. 61.

48 R. Collins, *Weberian Sociological Theory* (Cambridge: Cambridge University Press, 1988).

49 B. Russett, 'The Mysterious Case of Vanishing Hegemony; or Is Mark Twain Really Dead?', *International Organization*, Vol. 39 (1985); S. Strange, 'The Persistent Myth of Lost Hegemony', *International Organization*, Vol. 41 (1987).

50 J. Gowa, *Closing the Gold Window: Domestic Politics and the End of Bretton Woods* (Ithaca, NY: Cornell University Press, 1983).

51 The distinction between portfolio and multinational investment is clearly made by R. Gilpin, *US Power and the Multinational Corporation* (New York: Basic Books, 1975); see also *idem, The Political Economy of International Relations* (Princeton, NJ: Princeton University Press, 1987), Chapter 6.

52 Strange, 'The Myth of Lost Hegemony', pp. 566–71.

53 See Russett, 'The Mysterious Case of Vanishing Hegemony'. Gramscian theories of hegemony also stress the social and cultural dimensions of power; see R. Cox, 'Gramsci, Hegemony and International Relations: An Essay in Method', *Millennium*, Vol. 12 (1983), and *idem, Power, Production and World Order* (New York: Columbia University Press, 1987).

54 G. J. Ikenberry, 'Rethinking the Origins of American Hegemony', unpublished paper (1988); M. Mastanduno, 'Trade as a Strategic Weapon: American and Alliance Export Control Policy in the Early Postwar Period', *International Organization*, vol. 42 (1988); P.

Laurent, 'America's Ally, Britain's Opponent: Belgium and the OEEC/EPU Debates, 1947–50', *Millennium*, Vol. 16 (1987).

55 R. Aron, *Peace and War* (London: Weidenfeld and Nicolson, 1966).

56 D. Calleo 'The Historiography of the Interwar Trend: Reconsideration', in B. Rowland, ed., *Balance of Power or Hegemony?* (New York: New York University Press, 1975).

57 J. Goldstein, 'Ideas, Institutions, and American Trade Policy', *International Organization*, Vol. 42 (1988).

58 See G. J. Ikenberry, 'Conclusion: An Institutional Approach to American Foreign Economic Policy', *International Organization*, Vol. 42 (1988).

59 S. Krasner, 'Regimes and the Limits of Realism: Regimes as Autonomous Variables' in *idem*, ed., *International Regimes* (Ithaca, NY: Cornell University Press, 1984), pp. 359–61.

60 See S. Haggard and B. Simmons, 'Theories of International Regimes', *International Organization*, Vol. 41 (1987).

61 I. M. Destler and J. Odell, *Anti Protection: Changing Forces in United States Trade Politics* (Washington, DC: Institute for International Economics, 1987); H. Milner, 'Resisting the Protectionist Temptation: Industry and the Making of Trade Policy in France and the United States during the 1970s', *International Organization*, Vol. 41 (1987).

62 P. Kennedy, *The Rise and Fall of the Great Powers* (New York: Random House, 1988), Chapter 8.

63 R. Gilpin, 'American Policy in the Post-Reagan Era', *Daedalus*, Vol. 116 (1987).

64 D. Calleo, *Beyond Hegemony* (New York: Basic Books, 1988); S. Krasner, *Asymmetries in Japanese American Trade* (Berkeley: University of California Press, 1987).

65 K. Knorr, 'Burden-Sharing in NATO', *Orbis*, Vol. 29 (1985).

66 G. Treverton, *The 'Dollar Drain' and American Forces in Germany* (Athens, Ohio: Ohio University Press, 1978) is a particularly good study of this sort of phenomenon.

67 F. Bergsten and W. Cline, *The United States–Japan Economic Problem* (Washington, DC: Institute for International Economics, 1987).

68 S. Krasner, *Defending the National Interest* (Princeton, NJ: Princeton University Press, 1978); B. Moore, *Reflections on the Causes of Human Misery and upon Certain Proposals to Eliminate Them* (Boston: Beacon Press, 1977), Chapter 5; R. Aron, *Imperial Republic* (London: Weidenfeld and Nicolson, 1978).

69 A. J. Bender, 'Angola Challenges US Flexibility'; *New York Times*, 26 August 1987.

70 M. Mann, *States, War and Capitalism* (Oxford: Basil Blackwell, 1988).

71 R. Keohane, *After Hegemony* (Princeton, NJ: Princeton University Press, 1984).

Chapter 6

1 A. Gerschenkron, *Economic Backwardness in Historical Perspective* (Cambridge, MA: Harvard University Press, 1962), p. 44. Further variations are found by A. O. Hirschman among 'late, late' industrializers in 'The Political Economy of Import-Substituting Industrialization' in Hirschman, *A Bias for Hope* (New Haven, CT: Yale University Press, 1971).

2 G. J. Ikenberry, 'The Irony of State Strength: Comparative Responses to the Oil Shocks in the 1970s' *International Organization*, Vol. 40 (1986).

3 See R. Vernon, 'The International Aspects of State-Owned Enterprises', *Journal of International Business Studies*, Vol. 10 (1979).

4 Ikenberry, 'The Irony of State Strength'.

5 E. Gellner, *Relativism and the Social Sciences* (Cambridge: Cambridge University Press, 1986).

6 R. Aron, 'Reason, Passion and Power in the Thought of Clausewitz', *Social Research*, Vol. 39 (1972).

7 Montesquieu, *The Spirit of the Laws*, Part One, Chapter 3, cited in R. Aron, *Peace and War* (London: Weidenfeld and Nicolson, 1966), p. vii.

8 M. Doyle, 'Kant, Liberal Legacies and Foreign Affairs', *Philosophy and Public Affairs*, Vol. 12, nos 3 and 4 (1983).

9 We refer here to realist thinkers such as Kennan and Kissinger. Cf. M. J. Smith, *Realist Thought from Weber to Kissinger* (Baton Rouge: Louisiana State University Press, 1987).

10 R. Aron, *Clausewitz* (London: Routledge and Kegan Paul, 1984).

Select Bibliography

Adams, B., *The Law of Civilization and Decay* (New York: Alfred A. Knopf, 1943).

Anderson, P., *Lineages of the Absolutist State* (London: New Left Books, 1974).

Anderson, P., *Passages from Antiquity to Feudalism* (London: New Left Books, 1974).

Andreski, S., *Military Organization and Society* (Berkeley: University of California Press, 1971).

Aron, R., *Peace and War* (London: Weidenfeld and Nicolson, 1966).

Aron, R., *Democracy and Totalitarianism* (London: Weidenfeld and Nicolson, 1968).

Aron, R., *The Imperial Republic* (Englewood Cliffs, NJ: Prentice-Hall, 1974).

Aron, R., *Clausewitz* (London: Routledge and Kegan Paul, 1984).

Badie, B., and Birnbaum, P., *The Sociology of the State* (Chicago: University of Chicago Press, 1983).

Bean, R., 'War and the Birth of the Nation State', *Journal of Economic History*, Vol. 33 (1973).

Beitz, C., *Political Theory and International Relations* (Princeton, NJ: Princeton University Press, 1979).

Bendix, R., ed., *State and Society* (Berkeley: University of California Press, 1973).

Berger, S., *Peasants against Politics* (Cambridge, MA: Harvard University Press, 1972).

Berger, S., ed., *Organizing Interests in Western Europe* (Cambridge: Cambridge University Press, 1981).

Birnbaum, P., *The Heights of Power* (Chicago: University of Chicago Press, 1982).

Breuilly, J., *Nationalism and the State* (Manchester: Manchester University Press, 1986).

Bull, H., *The Anarchical Society* (New York: Columbia University Press, 1977).

Calleo, D. and B. Rowland, *America and the World Political Economy* (Bloomington: Indiana University Press, 1973).

Calleo, D., *Beyond Hegemony* (New York: Basic Books, 1987).

Carneiro, R. L., 'A Theory of the Origin of the State', *Science*, Vol. 169 (1970).

Carnoy, M., *The State and Political Theory* (Princeton, NJ: Princeton University Press, 1984).

Carr, E. H., *The Twenty Years' Crisis, 1919–1939* (London: Macmillan, 1951).

Claessen, H. and Skalnik, P., eds, *The Early State* (The Hague: Mouton, 1978).

Clastres, P., *Society Against the State* (New York: Basil Blackwell, 1977).

Cohen, B. J., *The Question of Imperialism* (New York: Basic Books, 1973).

Crone, P., *Slaves on Horses* (Cambridge: Cambridge University Press, 1980).

Crone, P., *Pre-Industrial Societies* (Oxford: Basil Blackwell, 1989).

Dahrendorf, R., *Society and Democracy in Germany* (New York: Anchor Books, 1969).

Doyle, M., 'Kant, Liberal Legacies and Foreign Affairs', *Philosophy and Public Affairs*, Vol. 12, nos 3 and 4 (1983).

Doyle, M., *Empires* (Ithaca, NY: Cornell University Press, 1986).

Dyson, K., *The State Tradition in Western Europe* (New York: Oxford University Press, 1980).

Eberhard, W., *Conquerors and Rulers* (Leiden: Brill, 1965).

Esping-Anderson, G., *Politics against Markets* (Princeton, NJ: Princeton University Press, 1985).

Evans, P. B., *Dependent Development* (Princeton, NJ: Princeton University Press, 1979).

Evans, P. B., Rueschemeyer, D. and Skocpol, T., *Bringing the State Back In* (New York: Cambridge University Press, 1985).

Feigenbaum, H. B., *Politics of Public Enterprise: Oil and the French State* (Princeton, NJ: Princeton University Press, 1985).

Freeman, J. R., *The Politics of Mixed Economics* (Ithaca, NY: Cornell University Press, 1988).

Friedman, D., *The Misunderstood Miracle* (Ithaca, NY: Cornell University Press, 1988).

Gaddis, J. L., *The United States and the Origins of the Cold War, 1941–47* (New York: Columbia University Press, 1972).

Gaddis, J. L., *Strategies of Containment* (Oxford: Oxford University Press, 1982).

Gaddis, J. L., *The Long Peace* (New York: Oxford University Press, 1987).

Gallie, W. B., *Philosophers of War and Peace* (Cambridge: Cambridge University Press, 1978).

Geary, D., *European Labour Protest, 1848–1945* (London: Methuen, 1984).

Geertz, C., *Negara* (Princeton, NJ: Princeton University Press, 1980).

Gellner, E., *Nations and Nationalism* (Oxford: Basil Blackwell, 1983).

Gellner, E., *Plough, Sword and Book* (London: Collins, 1988).

Gereffi, G., *The Pharmaceutical Industry and Dependency in the Third World* (Princeton, NJ: Princeton University Press, 1983).

Gerschenkron, A., *Economic Backwardness in Historical Perspective* (Cambridge, MA: Harvard University Press, 1962).

Gilbert, F., *To the Farewell Address* (Princeton, NJ: Princeton University Press, 1961).

Gilbert, F., ed., *The Historical Essays of Otto Hintze* (New York: Oxford University Press, 1975).

Gilpin, R., *U.S. Power and the Multinational Corporation* (New York: Basic, 1975).

Gilpin, R., *War and Change in World Politics* (New York: Cambridge University Press, 1981).

Gilpin, R., *The Political Economy of International Relations* (Princeton, NJ: Princeton University Press, 1987).

Goldthorpe, J., ed., *Order and Conflict in Western European Capitalism* (Oxford: Oxford University Press, 1984).

Gourevitch, P., *Politics in Hard Times* (Ithaca, NY: Cornell University Press, 1987).

Haas, E., *Beyond the Nation-State* (Stanford, CA: Stanford University Press, 1987).

Hall, J. A., *Powers and Liberties* (Harmondsworth: Penguin, 1986).

Hall, J. A., ed., *States in History* (Oxford: Basil Blackwell, 1986).

Hall, J. A., *Liberalism* (London: Paladin, 1988).

Hall, P., *Governing the Economy* (Oxford: Oxford University Press, 1986).

Hamilton, N., *The Limits of State Autonomy* (Princeton, NJ: Princeton University Press, 1982).

Hartz, L., *The Liberal Tradition in America* (New York: Harcourt, Brace and World, 1955).

Hinsley, F. H., *Power and the Pursuit of Peace* (Cambridge: Cambridge University Press, 1963).

Hirschman, A. O., *National Power and the Structure of Foreign Trade* (Berkeley: University of California Press, 1969).

Hirschman, A. O., *The Passions and the Interests* (Princeton, NJ: Princeton University Press, 1977).

Hoffman, S., *Primacy or World Order* (New York: McGraw-Hill, 1978).

Hoffmann, S., *Duties Beyond Borders* (Syracuse, NY: Syracuse University Press, 1981).

Holloway, J. and Picciotto, S., eds, *State and Capital* (London: Edward Arnold, 1978).

Howard, M., *War and the Liberal Conscience* (Oxford: Oxford University Press, 1978).

Huntington, S. P., *Political Order in Changing Societies* (New Haven, CT: Yale University Press, 1968).

Ikenberry, G. J., 'The Irony of State Strength: Comparative Responses to the Oil Shocks in the 1970s', *International Organization*, vol. 40 (1986).

Ikenberry, G. J., *Reasons of State* (Ithaca, NY: Cornell University Press, 1988).

Ikenberry, G. J., Lake, D. A. and Mastanduno, M., eds, *The State and American Foreign Economic Policy* (Ithaca, NY: Cornell University Press, 1988).

Janowitz, M., *The Military in the Political Development of New Nations* (Chicago: University of Chicago Press, 1964).

Jessop, B., *The Capitalist State* (New York: New York University Press, 1982).

Jessop, B., *Nicos Poulantzas* (London: Macmillan, 1985).

Jones, E. L., *The European Miracle* (Cambridge: Cambridge University Press, 1981).

Kaldor, M., *The Disintegrating West* (New York: Hill and Wang, 1978).

Katzenstein, P. J., ed., *Between Power and Plenty* (Madison: University of Wisconsin Press, 1978).

Katzenstein, P., *Small States in World Markets* (Ithaca, NY: Cornell University Press, 1985).

Kennedy, P., *The Rise of the Anglo German Antagonism, 1860–1914* (London: George Allen & Unwin, 1980).

Kennedy, P., *The Rise and Fall of the Great Powers* (New York: Random House, 1987).

Keohane, R., *After Hegemony* (Princeton, NJ: Princeton University Press, 1984).

Keohane, R., ed., *Structural Realism and Beyond* (New York: Columbia University Press, 1986).

Keohane, R., and Nye, J., *Power and Interdependence* (Boston: Little, Brown, 1977).

Keynes, J. M., *The Economic Consequences of the Peace* (London: Macmillan, 1919).

Kindleberger, C., *The World in Depression, 1919–1933* (Berkeley: University of California Press, 1973).

Kissinger, H. A., *A World Restored* (Boston: Houghton Mifflin, 1957).

Knorr, K., *The Power of Nations* (New York: Basic Books, 1975).

Krader, L., *Formation of the State* (Englewood Cliffs, NJ: Prentice-Hall, 1968).

Krasner, S., *Defending the National Interest* (Princeton, NJ: Princeton University Press, 1978).

Krasner, S., *Structural Conflict* (Berkeley: University of California Press, 1985).

Lane, F. C., *Venice and History* (Baltimore, MD: Johns Hopkins University Press, 1966).

Lehmbruch, G. and Schmitter, P. C., eds, *Patterns of Corporatist Policy-Making* (Beverly Hills, CA: Sage, 1982).

Levi, M., 'The Predatory Theory of Rule', *Politics and Society*, vol. 10 (1981).

Lindblom, C. E., *Politics and Markets* (New York: Basic, 1977).

List, F., *The National System of Political Economy* (Philadelphia: J. B. Lippincott, 1856).

Luttwak, E., *The Grand Strategy of the Roman Empire* (Baltimore, MD: Johns Hopkins University Press, 1976).

Maier, C., *In Search of Stability* (Cambridge: Cambridge University Press, 1987).

Mann, J. M., *The Sources of Social Power. Vol. 1: From the Beginning to 1760 AD* (Cambridge: Cambridge University Press, 1986).

Mann, M., *States, War and Capitalism* (Oxford: Basil Blackwell, 1988).

McNeill, W. H., *The Rise of the West* (Chicago: University of Chicago Press, 1963).

McNeill, W. H., *The Pursuit of Power* (Oxford: Basil Blackwell, 1982).

Miliband, R., *The State in Capitalist Society* (New York: Basic Books, 1969).

Modelski, G., 'Agraria and Industria: Two Models of the International System', *World Politics*, Vol. 14 (1961).

Montesquieu, C. L., *Considerations on the Causes of the Greatness of the Romans and Their Decline* (New York: Fress Press, 1965).

Moore, B., Jr., *Political Power and Social Theory* (New York: Harper and Row, 1965).

Moore, B., Jr., *Social Origins of Dictatorship and Democracy* (Boston: Beacon, 1966).

Morgenthau, H. J., *Politics among Nations* (New York: Alfred A. Knopf, 1973).

Mouzelis, N., *The Politics of the Semi-Periphery* (London: Macmillan, 1986).

Nettl, J. P., 'The State as a Conceptual Variable', *World Politics*, Vol. 20 (1968).

Nordlinger, E. A., *On the Autonomy of the Democratic State* (Cambridge, MA: Harvard University Press, 1981).

North, D. C. and Thomas, R. P., *The Rise of the Western World* (Cambridge: Cambridge University Press, 1973).

O'Connor, J., *The Fiscal Crisis of the State* (New York: St Martin's, 1973).

O'Donnell, G. P., Schmitter, P. C. and Whitehead, L., eds., *Transitions from Authoritarian Rule* (Baltimore, MD: Johns Hopkins Press, 1986).

Offe, C., 'Structural Problems of the Capitalist State', *German Political Studies*, Vol. 1 (1974).

Offe, C., *Disorganized Capitalism* (Cambridge, MA: MIT Press, 1985).

Okimoto, D. I., *Between MITI and the Market* (Stanford, CA: Stanford University Press, 1988).

Olson, M., *The Rise and Decline of Nations* (New Haven, CT: Yale University Press, 1982).

Oppenheimer, F., *The State* (New York: Free Life Editions, 1975).

Piore, M. J., and Sabel, C. F., *The Second Industrial Divide* (New York: Basic, 1984).

Poggi, G., *The Development of the Modern State* (London: Hutchinson, 1978).

Polanyi, K., *The Great Transformation* (Boston: Beacon Press, 1957).

Poulantzas, N., *Political Power and Social Classes* (London: New Left Books, 1973).

Poulantzas, N., *State, Power and Socialism* (London: New Left Books, 1978).

Rosecrance, R., *The Rise of the Trading State* (New York: Basic Books, 1986).

Samuels, R. J., *The Business of the Japanese State* (Ithaca, NY: Cornell University Press, 1987).

Schapiro, L., *Totalitarianism* (New York: Praeger, 1972).

Schmitter, P. C. and Lehmbruch, G., eds, *Trend toward Corporatist Intermediation* (Beverly Hills, CA: Sage, 1979).

Scott, J. C., *The Moral Economy of the Peasant* (New Haven, CT: Yale University Press, 1976).

Sen, G., *The Military Origins of Industrialisation and International Trade Rivalry* (London: Frances Pinter, 1984).

Service, E. R., *The Origins of the State and Civilization* (New York: Norton, 1975).

Skocpol, T., *States and Social Revolutions* (Cambridge: Cambridge University Press, 1979).

Skowronek, S., *Building a New American State* (New York: Cambridge University Press, 1982).

Smith, A., *The Wealth of Nations* (Oxford: Oxford University Press, 1976).

Smith, D., 'Domination and Containment', *Comparative Studies in Society and History*, Vol. 19 (1977).

Smith, M. J., *Realist Thought from Weber to Kissinger* (Baton Rouge: Louisiana State University Press, 1987).

Stepan, A., *The State and Society* (Princeton, NJ: Princeton University Press, 1978).

Strange, S., *Casino Capitalism* (Oxford: Basil Blackwell, 1986).

Strayer, J. R., *On the Medieval Origins of the Modern State* (Princeton, NJ: Princeton University Press, 1970).

Suleiman, E., *Private Power and Centralization in France* (Princeton, NJ: Princeton University Press, 1988).

Taylor, A. J. P., *The Trouble Makers* (London: Panther, 1969).

Therborn, G., *What Does the Ruling Class Do When it Rules?* (London: New Left Books, 1978).

Thucydides, *The Peloponnesian War* (New York: Modern Library, 1951).

Tilly, C., ed., *The Formation of National States in Western Europe* (Princeton, NJ: Princeton University Press, 1975).

Tocqueville, A. de, *The Old Regime and the French Revolution* (New York: Anchor Books, 1955).

Trimberger, E. K., *Revolution from Above* (New Brunswick, NJ: Transaction Books, 1978).

Veblen, T., *Imperial Germany and the Industrial Revolution* (New York: Viking Press, 1939).

Vernon, R., *Sovereignty at Bay* (New York: Basic Books, 1971).

Waisman, C., *Reversal of Development in Argentina* (Princeton, NJ: Princeton University Press, 1987).

Wallerstein, I., *The Modern World System* (New York: Academic Press, 1974).

Waltz, K. N., *Man, the State and War* (New York: Columbia University Press, 1959).

Waltz, K. N., *Theory of International Politics* (Reading, MA: Addison-Wesley, 1979).

Weber, M., *Economy and Society* (New York: Bedminster Press, 1968).

Weiss, L, *Creating Capitalism* (Oxford: Blackwell, 1988).

Wesson, R. G., *The Imperial Order* (Berkeley: University of California Press, 1967).

Wesson, R. G., *State Systems* (New York: Free Press, 1978).

Wight, M., *Systems of States* (Leicester: Leicester University Press, 1977).

Wight, M., *Power Politics* (London: Penguin Books, 1979).

Wiles, P. J., *Economic Institutions Compared* (New York: Wiley, 1977).

Winch, D., *Adam Smith's Politics* (Cambridge: Cambridge University Press, 1978).

Wolin, S. S., *Politics and Vision* (Boston: Little, Brown, 1960).

Wright, Q. A., *A Study of War* (Chicago: University of Chicago Press, 1942).

Index

1190